IN SEARCH OF
THE BEST SWEDISH CHOKLADBOLLAR

a southeast asian falls in love with *fika*

Alaine Handa

First published in Great Britain by Springtime Books

© Alaine Handa, 2018

All rights reserved. No part of this publication may be reproduced, stored in or introduced into a retrieval system or transmitted, in any form, or by any means (electronic, mechanical, photocopying, recording or otherwise) without the prior written permission from the publisher.

This book is sold subject to the condition that it shall not, by way of trade or otherwise, be lent, resold, hired out or otherwise circulated without the publisher's prior consent in any form of binding or cover other than in which it is published and without a similar condition including this condition being imposed on the subsequent purchaser.

ISBN: 978-1-9997323-5-6

Photo courtesy of Visit Lund; Photo Credit K. Saether on page 137.

Cover, interior page design and certain photos by Pierre Orsander
www.orsander.com

innehåll
table of contents

sum of all parts = chokladbollar

foreword	9
love at first bite	11
about alaine	13
dive into fika	14
basic ingredients	27
simple tools	32

recipes

boozy	37
classic	51
fruit	61
nut	79
holiday	89
world	99

profiles

stockholm	115
gothenburg	123
helsingborg	131
lund	137
malmö	143
bloggers	147
glossary of swedish fika terms	152
acknowledgements	156
index	158

foreword

For the love of chocolate and passion for cacao, from the cocoa farmers to the kitchen. This cookbook by Alaine is for those who enjoy making delicious morsels in the kitchen using great ingredients. Both of us are chocoholics from Southeast Asia and want to share with the world why eating good quality chocolate is beneficial to humanity, community, and the planet.

Indonesia is the third largest producer of cocoa beans in the world. Cocoa is grown throughout the archipelago from Aceh to Papua, and touches the lives of over a million farmers. Through the world of craft chocolate, Krakakoa has been working with farmers to experiment with fermentation and drying techniques that bring out the best flavors possible from Indonesian beans. Training, high premiums, and a focus on sustainable farming practices have been key to producing cocoa beans that are not only high in quality, but also have positive impacts on the planet, and the people who grow them.

When Alaine contacted me, she told me how she picked up a canister of our Krakakoa drinking chocolate and used it in some of her recipes for Swedish *chokladbollar*. Chocolate is the perfect complement with a cup of coffee, and the Swedish coffee culture of *Fika* – focus on taking time out of one's day to reconnect with each other and ourselves – in some ways mirrors the philosophy we have at Krakakoa about chocolate production. I hope that through the recipes in this book, and in the process of enjoying the treats you create, you will find opportunities to connect the chocolate in your hands to the people around you.

Sabrina Mustopo, Krakakoa chocolate
www.krakakoa.com

love at first bite

The first time I tried a *chokladbollar* was many years ago while I was still living in New York City (NYC). A new coffee spot called *Fika* opened in my neighborhood and I remembered that *fika* was a Swedish version of taking afternoon tea, but instead of tea, coffee was the preferred beverage. I had studied Swedish in college and taken a number of classes at the Scandinavian studies department so I was intrigued to step into this tiny cafe.

The *chokladbollar* reminded me of the rumballs I had grown up with as a child in Jakarta. My aunt used to make them with real rum, lots of butter, and chocolate. I was pleasantly surprised at the taste of the *chokladbollar* – they were so similar, and yet different. Deliciously rich in chocolate, they were a bit grainy, with dark earthy tones that paired well with my black coffee.

How I learned to make *chokladbollar*

On one of my many long haul flights from Copenhagen to Singapore, I sat next to a lovely young Swedish woman on her way 'home' to Australia. We chatted a little in Swedish and I ended up telling her about my love for *chokladbollar*. She told me the balls were easy to make and revealed the recipe there and then; I scribbled it excitedly into my notebook.

After several years and countless batches of trial and error attempts, I am now able to make *chokladbollar* that I can actually describe as "pretty damn good." I have also experimented with different ingredients typical of a specific location for example, *kaya* jam is used in my dairy-free and vegan recipes. *Kaya* is a coconut jam usually found in Singapore and Malaysia. Making the best *chokladbollar* is an obsession of mine and it brings me great joy when friends and family are able to join me for a *fika* and taste test my latest seven creations. I hope you enjoy my *chokladbollar* journey, recipes, and stories.

Alaine Handa

about alaine

Equipped with a BA in World Arts and Cultures from the University of California, Los Angeles, a postgraduate in Hospitality Management from Les Roches International School of Hospitality Management Switzerland, and wine certificates from Wine Spirits Education Trust London, Alaine has a creative global soul.

A picky eater with an active imagination, Alaine was offered wonderful food from all over the world by her grandmother, exposing her to spices, flavors, exotic smells, and most importantly, the freshest ingredients. Growing up between worlds, she is used to crossing multiple cultures and countries.

Born in Singapore, Alaine had her young childhood years in Jakarta and then grew up in Singapore in the expat world, with summers in Sydney and California to visit her relatives. She later went on to live for more than a decade in the US, graduate school in the Swiss Alps, and worked in Brussels. She now splits her time between Singapore and Europe.

A bonafide global citizen (or your average Third Culture Kid), Alaine straddles the gap between worlds. Hybrid cuisines and cultures, multicultural ambiguities, international communities and cross-cultural chameleons are commonplace features of her mixed up life. Through diverse careers as a professional contemporary dancer and choreographer, education, events, hospitality, food and beverage, and tourism, she's had a colorful background. Her hyper-creative brain never stops spinning and she's always either creating new recipes or choreographing new dances in her head.

Alaine loves to host dinner parties and *fika* afternoons with friends. Being busy in the kitchen and creating delicious somethings for others to enjoy never ceases to put a smile on her face. Once she started adopting *fika* as a way of life and enjoying a weekly *chokladbollar*, she wanted to share that small slice of joy with others. The journey of the *chokladbollar* for Alaine was more than a simple treat. It became a way of life, a way of *fika*, and a way of embracing 'just the right amount' or *lagom*.

www.travelwithalaine.com

dive into fika

Chokladbollar (pronounced *hocklardbollaar*) are Swedish chocolate balls. Irresistible morsels of chocolate the Swedes make after school with their *mormor* or *farmor* (mother's mother or father's mother – in other words, their grandmothers). They are love at first bite.
Trust me, once you've tried a really good *chokladboll* you will want to eat these semi-healthy chocolate balls all the time.

ingredients

The basic ingredients for classic *chokladbollar* are so simple they could only be Swedish:

oats
butter
sugar
vanilla sugar
salt
cocoa
coffee

typical toppings: shaved coconut or pearl sugar

Yes, that's it!

a history lesson

From humble beginnings, chokladbollar – or the Danish equivalent *havregrynskugle* were made popular in Sweden and Denmark during the Second World War. Leftover ingredients were used to make tasty little morsels composed of oats, coffee, cocoa, sugar and butter.

Originally, they were known as *negerboll* (negro ball). In 2006, the *Svenska Akademiens Ordlista* (the Swedish equivalent of the Oxford English Dictionary) changed the name to chokladboll. For obvious reasons, using the original term will probably result in the person being corrected to chokladboll or chokladbollar. When I ask Swedes about this, they tell me stories of older generations coming in to order negerbollar and how they would correct them, not only because of the racist connotations of using the word 'negro', but also due to the rising popularity of chokladbollar of various colors, meaning that 'chokladbollar' is a more inclusive term.

Still a favorite treat among school-aged children and adults, chokladbollar today are found at many children's parties, fika events, bakeries, and cafés throughout Sweden and Denmark. If you ask any Swede, they'll probably tell you a story about learning to make chokladbollar at home with their family and how they in turn went to pass on the tradition to their own children or grandchildren.

two words you need to know

The Swedes have a word for everything that is on trend at the moment.
Let me introduce you to two of them:

lagom

Lagom is a super Swedish word that's gaining so much traction the world is starting to take notice. It kind of means 'not too much, not too little, but just the right amount.' Lagom describes the Swedish way of life to a T.

Unsurprisingly, chokladbollar are all about lagom. You simply choose your ingredients and how much to use of each according to your own taste and preference. Not too much, not too little: lagom! The amounts you choose will depend on the size of the balls, the temperature of your kitchen and the flavor you're going for. And let's not forget that obligatory ingredient: love.

There's no doubt that when you use your hands instead of a spoon and feel the unctuous velvetiness on your skin, it's impossible not to derive more than a little pleasure from the process. Chocolate is both an aphrodisiac and a pick-me-up, so embrace the chance to get down and dirty in the kitchen. And best of all – these balls are 'semi-healthy'!

Making something with your palms and fingers is a tactile and visceral experience, even therapeutic. My favorite time to make chokladbollar is on days when I'm feeling overwhelmed. The simple act of repurposing my flagging energy into cooking up something yummy to share with others lifts my spirits up out of the doldrums. Most chokladbollar take less than 20 minutes to make from scratch and do not require any fancy equipment. You can, if you prefer, use a bowl and wooden spoon or a blender. I prefer to create mine in a large bowl using a wooden spoon to mix the dough before rolling the balls on a cool granite work surface dusted with a little icing sugar. Once the balls are in the fridge I lean back against the counter and lick the spoon or find a willing friend to help me 'clean' the bowl. What's not to like?

Go into any café or supermarket in Sweden and you'll find a fragrant and tantalizing array of chokladbollar or *delicatobollar*. Delicatobollar, meaning 'delicate' are a prepackaged brand sold in convenience stores and supermarkets. The chokladbollar you find in Swedish cafés tend to be smoother and more blended than mine. You can blend your chokladbollar with a fancy electric mixer like they do but out of ease, I make my chokladbollar without and share them with my friends around the world as homemade gifts all the time.

This book is all about minimalism, so the recipes you'll find here are simple to make and, apart from a large bowl, wooden spoon, a tray and a refrigerator, you hold all you need in the palm of your hands. Chokladbollar are fun to make (and to eat) for the whole family. You'll never be stuck for a snack, a *petit four*, teatime treat, dessert or gift again!

Come with me and we'll make some chokladbollar. If you're anything like me it'll be love at first bite! Whether you eat chokladbollar with your hands or slice away daintily with fork and knife, there's no wrong way to eat this fun little treat.

fika

The Swedes have an equivalent to the British afternoon tea break but instead of tea they drink a coffee. Swedish offices and companies are known to have mandated fika breaks in the afternoon. Typically lasting about an hour, fika is best taken with friends, family or colleagues. Swedes take their *fikapaus* to reset, and it's a really good chance not to have to think or talk about work. Fika is a moment to reflect and to come back to the present moment. I didn't grow up with the tradition but have adopted taking fika breaks most days. Most of the time I take fikapaus on my own with a cup of black coffee, paired with a little piece of chocolate. My favorite kind of fikapaus is with friends, sharing a piece of cake. It's important to take a mid-afternoon break to recharge and reconnect with people. Some workplaces in Sweden have made fikor mandatory (plural for fika) and so it's often not an option to not take a break.

You can have a fika break at home, in a café or in a park; something sweet washed down with a cup of black filter coffee is the perfect pairing for fika. Coffee is the traditional beverage of choice but you can also have fika with tea, juice or wine. Fika is a state of being, a culture, a tradition, a meditation, and a yummy one at that!

Chokladbollar come in different sizes, from small truffle-sized balls to those the size of a softball. My favorite size of chokladbollar is a small to medium palm-sized ball with rich dark cocoa and coffee flavors. Not too sweet, not too bitter – just right. Or, shall we say lagom. Lagom, as explained earlier, is a Swedish word for 'all things in balance.'

Other traditional cakes can be chocolate *kladdkaka, prinsesstårta, kanelbulle*, or the tradition of serving seven different kinds of mini butter cookies or cakes, known as *sju sorterskakor*, and typically consisting of *Brysselkex, chokladsnitt, dröm, Finska pinnar, hallongrotta, kanelkaka*, and *mandel mussla*. But you can mix in any combination as long as there are seven varieties.

Fika is about indulging in making time for a coffee break, either with friends or by yourself.

"Going for a fika at a 'fik' is a very Swedish thing. Fika basically means to meet up for a coffee and a piece of cake or pastry, and fik is slang for café, bakery or pastry shop. Sweden enjoys a highly developed culture when it comes to baked goods, and everywhere in Stockholm you'll find cafés and cake shops brimming with atmosphere, character, and quality, whether traditional or contemporary-creative."

Visit Stockholm

the bizarre history of fika

The word fika is slang, derived from reversing *kaffi*, a 19th century term for coffee, and used to refer to the act of taking a social coffee break with something to eat (usually cake). Sweden is one of the world's largest consumers of coffee, along with Finland and The Netherlands. Coffee arrived in Sweden in the mid 1670s and was popular among the wealthy classes. In 1746, the king placed a hefty and unpopular tax on coffee which led to the development of a prohibition-style black market for its sale and consumption.

But there was no stopping the Swedes from drinking their beloved beverage. King Gustav III feared the political consequences of these coffee meetings and their potential to harbor resistance to his rule so he sought to dissuade the public through fear-mongering and the dissemination of anti-coffee propaganda. He even went so far as to arrange an experiment whereby a pair of twins condemned to death were given the option of life imprisonment if they agreed to be a part of the experiment instead. One twin had to drink three pots of tea while the other had to drink three pots of coffee daily for the rest of their lives. Ironically, the king was assassinated before the results were concluded – the twin who drank tea died first while the one who drank coffee outlived them both.

how to host a beautiful fika at home

I've always loved having a few friends over for dinner or afternoon tea, and since incorporating fika into my life for the past decade, having people over for a coffee and small bites has become a no-brainer. Fika is not as formal or elaborate a dinner party as Thanksgiving for example, and impromptu *fikor* are pretty common and tend to be more informal, but I still like making my guests happy.

Something sweet, something salty, and loads of coffee!

During holidays, I like hosting dinners or small little parties as a way to celebrate the season, and especially to cheer people up when it's winter. It's also a chance for me to give homemade gifts to the people I care about. Several years ago, when I lived in New York, a close friend of mine came over on a cold winter's day and we spent the whole day in my kitchen making holiday sweets. We made peppermint bark, cookies, fudge, peanut brittle and placed them in beautiful tins. We laughed at our mishaps, spent quality time together, and made delicious confections. I would give away these tins of edibles as gifts and the people receiving them would be so touched that I vowed to always make homemade gifts or host dinner parties in lieu of giving actual gifts. The environmental impact of all that plastic, packaging, paper, and the wasteful culture of consumption is hurting us all in the long term.

Whether friends are old or new, the holiday season is for simple gatherings and quality time.

In order to have a balanced spread for a fika event, you should serve a combination of sweet treats like chokladbollar and savory items like crackers and cheese. For a fika holiday party in Singapore, I made a couple of pitchers of homemade iced tea with fresh herbs and steeped tea bags overnight, as well as a fresh pot of coffee. A month later, for a fika event in Malmö, I served seven different kinds of chokladbollar, sliced cucumber, Singaporean chilli dip, and some pork jerky. It's about balance in the snacks served but also about the company. Fika is about staying present and connecting (or reconnecting) with the people attending.

Sju sorters kakor, or seven different kinds of cookies, cakes, or even bread, is one of the most traditional of Swedish customs and one that is making a comeback. Often, when imbibing multiple cups of coffee with Swedes and non-Swedes, the discussion of cultural traditions comes up. It strikes me that many different cultures have a version of fika, often embedded in your childhood memories. For example, going to your grandmother's house on a Sunday afternoon for tea and cake is something many British people have experienced growing up, just as the Swedes go to their grandmother's house for fika and the seven cookies, cakes, or *fikabröd* (fika bread), all served with coffee, tea, or juice. I remember having Sunday afternoon tea almost every week after going to church with my mother in Singapore or going to my great aunt's house for an afternoon of baking and playtime with my cousins. Either way, it was a special time to recharge and relax.

the essential components of a successful fika:

- Serve seven different kinds of cookies, fikabröd, or cakes.
  If they're Swedish then all the better!
- Create a calm and cozy environment.
  Fika is a relaxing time to slow down and be present.
- Add some fresh flowers and candles to make things a little bit special.
- 'Homemade' goes a long way.
- Choose a combination of sweet and savory snacks.
- Serve freshly brewed coffee. When your guests arrive, offer them a cup of coffee. But, if your guests prefer tea, have a selection of caffeinated or non-caffeinated teas available too. You can also make homemade iced tea a few hours before with fresh mint leaves, lemon, loads of ice, and your favorite tea.
- Keep it informal. Fika is not like British afternoon tea. During summer months or in tropical climates, you might want to have your fika outdoors or, if it's too hot, keep your guests cool by making sure there's a fan or air conditioning, drinks, and make sure to serve food that's not too heavy.

One of my favorite activities when abroad is to stop at a café and take a fikapaus to recharge and watch passersby. It's a nice cultural activity to observe how people behave. Do they rush around and live in their own little bubbles, or do they do as the Swedes do and get a cup of coffee with a little sweet snack and sit down?

basic ingredients

Always find the best cocoa to make chokladbollar.

There's a basic list of ingredients to make classic chokladbollar. Let me explain in a little more depth about each important basic ingredient.

cacao

- *cocoa*
- *cacao*

You decide what you want to call it. Either way, it's probably the most important ingredient.

To get that rich chocolate color and flavor, you must get the best cocoa that you can find. For me, the darker the better because dark cocoa powder has more depth of flavor. Bitter, earthy notes, and sometimes hints of floral perfume mark a good cocoa. Biting into a chokladboll made with a darker cocoa counteracts the sweetness from the sugar.

I like chocolate desserts that have a complexity and richness to the flavor, more than just a basic sweet note that can feel harsh on the tongue.

Earthy, sweet, bitter, coffee-flavored, a hint of salt, and a hint of nuttiness.

These are the flavors I go for in my classic chokladbollar recipe.

van houten cacao powder
Origin: Amsterdam

This Dutch brand of cocoa powder is very dark and great for making chokladbollar, cakes, and hot cocoa drinks. When I was living in Brussels, I would make chokladbollar almost every week to bring to the office and that's when I discovered this brand. It's packaged in an unassuming box and was placed next to a lot of other specialty cocoa powders. The Belgians are very serious about their chocolate! I didn't have a large budget at the time, so I picked up the most basic cocoa powder I could find. Little did I know it would become one of the brands that I would actively seek out in the future. The chocolate balls I rolled in my tiny apartment kitchenette were some of the best chokladbollar I've ever made!

Taste: Dark, earthy, coffee-flavored, with a hint of creamy floral notes.

fazer cacao
Origin: Finland

You'll find this staple cacao powder in every Scandinavian cupboard (hot cocoa winter nights are the cosiest!). It's also a really good one for making chokladbollar because it's dark and pretty good quality for a basic cocoa powder. The chokladbollar I've made with this have consistently had a rich dark chocolate flavor finish with just the right amount of sweetness.

Unfortunately, this cocoa powder is fairly hard to find outside of Scandinavia and may be sold only in specialty Scandinavian food shops. I make chokladbollar with Fazer Cacao powder in Scandinavia because it's a classic and traditional.

Taste: Dark, earthy, sweet, and a hint of coffee flavor.

be a cocoa hunter
I hoard specialty cacoa products!

When traveling or living in a new country, I like spending time searching for specialty chocolate shops and purchasing specialty cacao and chocolate for my chokladbollar. After living in Switzerland and Belgium, a chocolate lover's dream, I tried all kinds of cocoa powders and different chocolate products to add to my recipes. It was a bit geeky, but each time I experimented, there would be a new discovery. Currently in my pantry I have cacao powder from Italy, France, The Netherlands, Vietnam, Indonesia, Sweden, England and Switzerland.

In addition to a good basic cocoa powder, it's important to experiment with different types of cocoa powder. Basic chokladbollar recipes are simple and baking at home should be fun, so have a little fun trying out different powders! The more you add into the mixture, the more depth of flavor the balls will have. I like my balls to have a bit of complexity.

It is important to note the kind of style and flavor of chokladbollar you want to make. Do you want more of a milk chocolate, white chocolate, dark chocolate, or a mix of all the above? You don't have to stick to just one cacao powder for each batch of chokladbollar you make. I like to experiment a little and mix two to three different cacao powders in a single mix. By doing this you create a depth in flavor.

coffee
Kaffe, kopi, koffie, café, cup of joe...
Coffee is important for making for making awesome chokladbollar.

One of the primary ingredients in Swedish chokladbollar is coffee. Swedes love drinking coffee, as demonstrated in the fika culture of taking several coffee breaks a day. I love taking a mid-afternoon fika to recharge and to give me that much needed caffeine jolt. The 'afternoon slump' is a condition that affects many of us. Swedes are rated as one of the top countries in the world in terms of coffee consumption.

Nothing is paired better with a cup of black coffee than a chokladbollar on the side...

Chokladbollar utilize coffee as a basic ingredient and that dark earthy note you get from biting into a chokladboll is its signature flavor.

how to make your coffee
Ways to prepare coffee for chokladbollar:

- Filter coffee: This is the most basic way to make your coffee ready for adding to chokladbollar. Most people make it this way.
- French press: Steep your coffee in boiling water before plunging.
- Moka pot: The traditional Italian way. I make my coffee at home using a moka pot almost every day. Once the coffee bubbles up to the top, make sure to remove it from the stove immediately to prevent your coffee and your moka pot from burning!
- Espresso: If you have a proper coffee machine at home, make an espresso and add that to your chokladbollar recipe – the result is dark chocolate heaven!
- Instant coffee: This is my least favorite way of making coffee but sometimes you don't have so much choice. Add a couple of teaspoons and mix well.
- Drip coffee: When you have the patience, this is the most elegant way to prepare coffee. I always order drip coffee at specialty cafés because the flavors and subtle nuances of the coffee really shine through.
- Nespresso: This global brand is taking home brew by storm. I would recommend making the coffee for your chokladbollar using the espresso method.

You can of course make your coffee however you like it. Experimentation makes cooking, like life, fun, and is a creative way to bring out different flavors.

temperature
The temperature of the coffee matters.

Like Goldilocks said: "not too hot, not too cold, just right." In other words: lagom.

I have experimented with different coffee temperatures for my chokladbollar recipes. Many Swedes swear by adding cold coffee. I prefer cool, almost room temperature coffee that has been sitting out for a while because of the different climates I work in. If the environment is too dry, the cold coffee does not absorb properly into the mixture. Too humid and the cold coffee doesn't bring out the coffee flavors into the mix.

butter

smör (pronounced 'smur' in Sweden but known as butter to most of us) is liberally used in traditional chokladbollar recipes as a binding agent and to keep the mixture indulgent and smooth. Though butter's gotten a bad reputation over the decades as a fat, I believe that all things in moderation will not be 'bad for you'. Butter is a natural source of fat and we all know we should eat more natural foods and make foods from scratch so we know exactly what we put into our bodies. My preferred butter of choice will always be organic salted butter. The Danish organic Lurpak works pretty well for making chokladbollar.

coconut oil, the vegan alternative

A lot of my recipes can be made vegan, dairy-free, gluten-free, and nut-free (excluding the specifically nutty balls, of course). Exchanging butter for virgin coconut oil and melted dark chocolate makes for a delicious plant-based alternative to dairy. I'm lactose intolerant and cannot handle milk or cream products without feeling sick but, for some reason, butter doesn't affect me. However, exploring the world of dairy-free and vegan desserts has led to exciting experiments for me in the kitchen. If you're throwing a fika party at home, or making chokladbollar for a bake sale, you never know whether someone might be lactose intolerant and/ or vegan so it might be a safer bet to use coconut oil as opposed to butter so more people can enjoy your chokladbollar.

oats

Natural, low in cholesterol, filling, healthy, high in fiber, versatile, and nutritious: oats are the main ingredient in Swedish chokladbollar and are what sets them apart from all the other chocolate balls of the world. I've a secret to tell you: I don't like eating oatmeal. *Shh…* I do love granola, oatmeal raisin cookies, and Swedish chokladbollar though! I take every chance I get to add more healthy fiber in my diet, especially when it tastes so good, tricking my picky taste buds into eating healthier foods. For chokladbollar, try to use quick oats or oat bran because the oats will be finer in texture and, as these balls are not baked, they will be easier to digest as well.

sugar

Muscovado raw brown sugar is my preferred ingredient for making chokladbollar and I love its earthiness and molasses-like texture. Muscovado is thought to be a healthier alternative to white refined sugar and it retains more mineral content from the sugar cane juice. It's very dark brown and slightly coarser and stickier than most brown sugars. It offers good resistance to high temperatures and has a reasonably long shelf life.

Traditional chokladbollar recipes use white and icing sugar, so you can use those, or mix different sugars to alter the level of sweetness in your chokladbollar mixtures. I use white and icing sugars in my white chokladbollar recipes.

simple tools

a large mixing bowl
measuring cups
a wooden spoon
a tablespoon
a teaspoon
a plate or tray
a small plate or small bowl
your hands!

Most Swedish children learn to make chokladbollar using these simple tools. It is the very first thing that children learn to make with their grandmothers, fathers, aunts and mothers because it doesn't require fancy tools or even baking. I like how simple these balls are to make and how many variations of chokladbollar there are. I also like to take fancy kitchen equipment out of the equation, which makes things even simpler. I've made chokladbollar in commercial kitchens, tiny kitchens without an oven, and in hotel rooms while traveling to give my friendly hosts some homemade gifts.

Important note: Always make sure you have short nails, clean hands, and if you're making them for a large group of people, its best to get some disposable gloves for sanitary purposes!

recipes

important note

When you start making chokladbollar the most important element you need to take in to account is the temperature of your environment. If the temperature is dry you may need to add more liquid; if it's humid your mixture may seem a little wet and will be easier to form into balls if you pop it in the fridge for a bit first.

Kneading your mixture after you've mixed all the wet and dry ingredients together will ensure you achieve the right lagom consistency. You want the mix to be not too dry, not too wet, and sticky enough so you can form the balls in your hands. Too wet – add more oats. Too dry – add more wet ingredients like butter or coffee, tea, juice or water.

boozy

Every country has its own age limit for the consumption of alcohol.
Please ensure that these chokladbollar are enjoyed in moderation.

black forest cherry

One of my favorite cakes as a child was black forest gateau drenched in cherry liquor (under the strict supervision of my aunt and mother). The combination of cream, chocolate cake, cherry kirsch and candied cherries, garnished with chocolate flakes was unimaginably delectable to my young self and there are countless pictures of me stuffing my face with the cake to prove it. Over the years, my taste for candied cherries has waned and I now prefer fresh black cherries. When it was cherry season, the farmers' markets and cherry sellers were on almost every other street corner in Manhattan and I would guzzle fresh black cherries until my lips were stained with a semi-permanent garnet color. This recipe can be made with cherry kirsch (a cherry liquor), cherry wine, or – for a non-alcoholic version – cherry juice. You can make your own cherry juice by crushing the cherries then straining the skins, adding filtered water and sugar.

makes about 12 small balls

300 ml oats
100 ml raw brown sugar
50 ml icing sugar
15 ml vanilla sugar or vanilla essence
100 ml cocoa powder
25 g organic salted butter
pinch of sea salt
100 ml dark chocolate chips
30-45 ml cold cherry liquor or cherry wine
3 cherries, stoned and quartered

garnish with...cocoa powder, icing sugar, chocolate sprinkles, or pearl sugar

Place the cherries in the freezer while you make the mixture for the balls. When you're ready to stuff the balls with the cherries, the cold cherries will be less sticky than if you had used fresh cherries.

Melt the butter and chocolate in a small saucepan over a low heat. Set aside to cool.

In a large bowl, mix the oats, sugar, vanilla sugar, icing sugar, sea salt and cocoa powder. Mix well with a wooden spoon and your hands, breaking up any clumps.

Add the cherry liquor and mix well with your hands. 30 ml of cherry liquor should be enough if you only want a hint but you'll need at least 45 ml if you want the cherry liquor aftertaste.

Slowly fold in half the melted butter and the chocolate into the mixture. Mix well with your hands. Now add the second half.

Using a tablespoon, take a scoop from the mix and place it in the palm of your hand. Form a ball and set aside on a tray or plate or a tray. Repeat.

Take the cherries out of the freezer.

Take a ball in your palm and with your thumb make an indentation in the middle of the ball. Put a cherry into each ball. Fold, mold, reform, and roll the balls.

On a separate plate, roll the balls in icing sugar until the entire ball is coated in sugar.

Store in the fridge for about an hour before serving.

boozehound whisky bourbon balls

Whisky and chocolate go really well together. Those chocolates you get at duty free with a little bit of spirit in them are some of my favorite treats. There's something about the little bit of alcohol in chocolate like a rum ball, black forest gateau, tiramisu or rum raisin ice cream that creates a warming sensation in the throat that's just so comforting, or as the Swedes like to say, *mysigt*. If you're under the legal drinking age though, you'll have to wait until your birthday to make these!

makes about 14 balls

300 ml oats
100 ml raw brown sugar
15 ml vanilla bean powder or 1 vanilla bean scraped
100 ml cocoa powder
30 ml organic salted butter
100 ml dark chocolate chips
45 ml of your favorite whisky or bourbon
pinch of sea salt

garnish with… cocoa powder or icing sugar

Melt the butter in a saucepan until slightly browned. Remove the saucepan from the heat and melt the dark chocolate chips by stirring in the chips with a wooden spoon. Add 15 ml of whisky and stir well. Set aside to cool.

In a large bowl, mix the oats, sugar, vanilla bean, cocoa powder, and sea salt. Blend all the ingredients well with your hands.

Add your favorite whisky or bourbon into the dry ingredients and mix well.

Slowly fold the melted butter, dark chocolate, and whisky or bourbon into the dry ingredients. Mix thoroughly with your hands and knead it so that it has a sticky consistency but is not wet. If it still feels too wet, add more oats and keep mixing and kneading with your hands until the oats are completely mixed in.

In a small bowl, pour some cocoa powder or icing sugar for the topping.

Using a tablespoon, take a scoop from the mix and place it in the palm of your hand. Form a ball and set aside on a tray or plate. Repeat.

Place your garnish of choice into a small bowl. Take a ball and drop it into the garnish, rolling until coated.

Place the balls in the fridge for about an hour. Now is also a good time to enjoy a neat whisky while you wait for the balls to be ready!

danish rum balls (*rømkugle*)

The Danes have a slight variation on their rum balls – instead of using crushed cookies or oats, leftover pound cake is used and thus creates the base for the rum balls. Cinnamon, hazelnuts or dried fruit may be added to the mix, creating a *rømkugle* that isn't quite as soft as the ones you find in Denmark.

makes 10 balls

500 ml leftover pound cake (plain sponge or Madeira cake)
100 ml cocoa powder
4 tbsp raspberry jam or strawberry jam
15 ml hazelnuts chopped
5 ml cinnamon
15 ml raisins
3 tbsp dark rum

garnish with… coconut or chocolate sprinkles

In a large bowl, crumble the leftover cake the size of cornflakes.

Add the cocoa powder, jam, hazelnuts, cinnamon, raisins, rum and mix well with your hands. Knead and form the mixture until the right consistency.

Using a tablespoon, take a scoop from the mix and place it in the palm of your hand. Form a ball and set aside on a tray or plate. Repeat.

Place your garnish of choice into a small bowl. Take a ball and drop it into the garnish, rolling until coated.

Store in the fridge for about an hour before serving.

aunt mona's rum balls

My late Aunt Mona used to make the most delectable rum balls and they were one of my favorite childhood treats. She was an amazing home baker and made rum balls of condensed milk, crushed Marie biscuits, cocoa powder, chocolate, butter, sugar, vanilla and rum. Rum essence may be used but the best part about rum balls is the warming aftertaste. I really like the combination of chocolate and dark rum. Because this recipe uses biscuits and not oats, the proportion of liquids should be measured carefully so the mixture doesn't get soggy and hard to form or roll into balls. Aunt Mona's rum balls were what got me hooked on eating chocolate balls and which led to my discovery of Swedish chokladbollar.

makes about 15 balls

300 ml crushed Marie biscuits
30 g condensed milk
25 g butter or margarine
100 ml cocoa powder
100 ml white sugar
15 ml vanilla essence
30 ml dark rum

garnish with… chocolate sprinkles or cocoa powder

There are a few ways you can crush Marie biscuits. You can use a food processor but if you're making these while on the road, or if you have a minimalist kitchen, you can also crush the biscuits using a rolling pin (or empty wine bottle) and a Ziploc bag.

Place the biscuits in a Ziploc bag and lightly tap to break them up into small pieces. Roll the pin over the biscuit pieces until they're tiny and well ground.

In a large bowl, place the dry ingredients of crushed biscuits, cocoa powder, white sugar and blend well with a wooden spoon.

Fold the condensed milk, room temperature butter, vanilla essence, and dark rum into the large bowl of dry ingredients.

Mix well with your hands.

Using a tablespoon, take a scoop from the mix and place it in the palm of your hand. Form a ball and set aside on a tray or plate. Repeat.

Place your garnish of choice into a small bowl. Take a ball and drop it into the garnish, rolling until coated.

Store the rum balls in the fridge for at least an hour before serving.

alaine's araksbollar

In Sweden, rum balls are called *araksbollar* and in Denmark they're called *rømkugle*. The word *arak* in Indonesian literally means alcohol, so as a nod to my childhood in Jakarta, calling my rum balls the same as the Swedes do is a good fit. A twist on my aunt Mona's rum ball recipe, I swapped out condensed milk and crushed biscuits for extra rum and oats. I like my araksbollar to have the taste of rum in them. The extra rum creates a warming sensation on the back of the throat and offers soothing comfort on cold winter nights.

makes about 14 balls

300 ml oats
25 g butter
100 ml cocoa powder
100 ml brown sugar
45 ml dark rum
15 ml vanilla sugar or vanilla bean powder
5 ml cinnamon powder
2 tbsp melted dark chocolate (made from dark chocolate pieces)
a pinch of sea salt

garnish with… chocolate sprinkles or cocoa powder or icing sugar

In a large bowl, place the oats, brown sugar, vanilla sugar, sea salt, cinnamon and cocoa powder and mix really well with your hands.

Melt the butter in a saucepan until slightly browned. Browned butter will bring out the caramelized flavors of the cocoa and chocolate.

Melt the dark chocolate pieces in the microwave. Do this in 30 second increments so the chocolate doesn't burn.

Add the rum and melted chocolate to the dry ingredients and mix well with your hands.

Slowly fold in the melted browned butter to the mixture and mix well with a wooden spoon.

Let the mixture cool for a few minutes before mixing with your hands.

Using a tablespoon, take a scoop from the mix and place it in the palm of your hand. Form a ball and set aside on a tray or plate. Repeat.

Place your garnish of choice into a small bowl. Take a ball and drop it into the garnish, rolling until coated.

Set the balls in the fridge for about an hour before serving.

guinness balls

When you want a beer and chocolate at the same time… I am not really a beer drinker but I know many people are…. then this is the chokladbollar recipe for you. I was pleasantly surprised at the combination of the dark Irish brew and chocolate. So indulgent and rich in flavor, in fact that if you love Guinness beer and dark chocolate, you will probably love this.

makes about 14 balls

300 ml oats
100 ml raw brown sugar
15 ml vanilla bean powder or 1 vanilla bean stalk
100 ml cocoa powder
30 ml organic salted butter
100 ml dark chocolate chips
45 ml Guinness beer
pinch of sea salt

garnish with… cocoa powder or melted dark chocolate with some crunchy chocolate bits and pearl sugar

Melt the butter in a saucepan until slightly browned. Remove the saucepan from the heat and melt in the dark chocolate chips by stirring the chips with a wooden spoon. Set aside to cool.

In a large bowl mix the oats, sugar, vanilla bean, cocoa powder, and sea salt. Blend all the ingredients well with your hands.

Add the Guinness beer into the dry ingredients and mix well.

Slowly fold half of the melted butter and dark chocolate into the dry ingredients. Mix thoroughly with your hands and knead it so that it is the right consistency of stickiness but not wet. If it does feel too wet, add more oats and keep mixing and kneading with your hands until the oats are completely mixed in.

In a small bowl, pour the crunchy chocolate bits and pearl sugar for the topping.

Using a tablespoon for measure, scoop up the mixture into small palm-sized balls.

Dip the balls in the remaining butter and melted chocolate mixture until the entire ball is coated.

Tip: I recommend using cupcake paper cups to contain the chocolate balls and prevent them from sticking to the plate or tray when you place them in the fridge

Garnish each ball with the crunchy chocolate bits and pearl sugar.

Place the balls into the fridge for about an hour before serving. Now is also a good time to drink the rest of your beer while you wait for the balls to be ready!

classic

alaine's classic swedish chokladbollar recipe

This recipe took five long years of trial and error to perfect. *Varsågod!*

makes about 12-14 balls

300 ml oats
100 ml cocoa powder
100 ml raw brown sugar
30 g organic salted butter
30 ml cold coffee
15 ml vanilla sugar
1 tbsp chocolate spread or melted dark chocolate
pinch of seasalt

garnish with… desiccated coconut or pearl sugar (melted dark chocolate optional)

Place all dry ingredients in a large bowl and mix well.

Melt the butter in a saucepan until slightly browned.

Add the coffee and mix well.

Fold in the hot melted butter.
If the mixture's a bit too wet, add more oats.

Mix all ingredients thoroughly with your hands.

Chill the mixture in the fridge for about 30 minutes.

Using a tablespoon, take a scoop from the mix and place it in the palm of your hand. Form a ball and set aside on a tray or plate. Repeat.

Place your garnish of choice into a small bowl. Take a ball and drop it into the garnish, rolling until coated. (If you're using melted dark chocolate, roll the balls in the dark chocolate first and then roll the balls in the garnish).

Store the balls in the freezer for at least an hour before serving.

bougie balls

These are called bougie balls because the ingredients are a step above the classic chokladbollar recipe, with specialty ingredients. *Bougie is the slang term taken from the word *bourgeois*.

makes about 12-14 balls

300 ml oats
100 ml Valrhona[1] cocoa powder
100 ml raw brown sugar
30 g organic salted butter
30 ml cold espresso coffee
15 ml vanilla bean powder or 1 vanilla bean
1 tbsp dark chocolate spread
pinch of truffle sea salt
pinch of cinnamon

garnish with… desiccated coconut or pearl sugar

(Bougie balls are *almost* identical to the classic balls, but not quite).

Place all dry ingredients in a large bowl and mix well: oats, sugar, cocoa, sea salt.

Cut open the vanilla bean pod and scrape the vanilla into the bowl (or add vanilla bean powder). Mix well.

Melt the butter in a saucepan until slightly browned.

Add the espresso coffee and mix well.

Fold in the hot melted butter. If the mixture's a bit too wet, add more oats.

Mix all the ingredients thoroughly with your hands.

Chill the mixture in the fridge for about 30 minutes.

Fill a small bowl with the desiccated coconut (or pearl sugar).

Using a tablespoon, take a scoop from the mix and place it in the palm of your hand. Form a ball and set aside on a tray or plate. Repeat.

Place your garnish of choice into a small bowl. Take a ball and drop it into the garnish, rolling until coated.

Store the balls in the freezer for at least an hour before serving.

---

[1] *Valrhona is a French cocoa and can be found in specialty shops. If you can't manage to get your hands on this particular cocoa, then get the best and most luxurious brand you can find!*

vegan classic

I'm not vegan, but have many vegan friends. I tried a few different chokladbollar recipes for them using different coconut oils, coconut creams, a coconut jam, and coconut milk, but the flavor slightly overpowered the dark chocolate taste. After countless trials and errors, I'm proud to present you with the best classic vegan chokladbollar. Even if you're not vegan, you'll appreciate the balance of flavors between the dark, earthy chocolate and the rich, creamy coconut. I wouldn't recommend using pearl sugar as a garnish since it could make the balls a bit too sweet. As an alternative, sugar lovers can create a garnish using raw cane sugar with cinnamon, cardamom, and icing sugar.

makes about 12-14 balls

300 ml oats
100 ml cocoa powder
100 ml raw cane sugar
15 ml vanilla sugar
pinch of sea salt
20 g coconut oil
20 g dark baking chocolate
30 ml coffee (espresso preferable)
1 tbsp vegan coconut butter, cream or oil

garnish with… desiccated coconut or raw cane sugar with cinnamon, cardamom and icing sugar

Brew a single shot of espresso and set aside to cool.

In a large bowl, add the oats, cocoa powder, raw cane sugar, vanilla sugar, and sea salt. Combine with your hands, making sure all the ingredients are mixed well.

Heat the coconut oil and dark chocolate together in a small saucepan. Stir constantly to avoid burning the chocolate.

Slowly add the coffee to the dry ingredients, mixing well with a wooden spoon.

Fold in half the coconut oil and chocolate mixture to the dry ingredients. Set aside the other half for the garnish. Mix with a wooden spoon and then switch to working by hand.

Tip: Do not burn your fingers! I pour in the heated coconut oil and chocolate mixture very slowly, using a tablespoon, before you work it with your hands.

Using a tablespoon, take a scoop from the mix and place it in the palm of your hand. Form a ball and set aside on a tray or plate. Repeat.

Place your garnish of choice into a small bowl and set aside.

Dip the balls into the remaining coconut oil and chocolate mixture until coated all over.

Roll the balls in the garnish and place onto a plate.

Cool the balls in the fridge for at least one hour before serving.

classic white

This recipe is dedicated to all the people who love the decadence of creamy white chocolate. It took me over one year to find the best way to make a white chokladbollar that really capitalizes on the creaminess of white chocolate without becoming too sickly sweet. White chocolate is a tricky thing, bringing with it two challenges: not only is it hard to keep the balls looking white but also its high milk content curdles easily when you heat it up. My white chocolate balls are also the only recipes where I use white sugar instead of my preferred raw cane sugar. In addition, I use a white vanilla powder instead of cocoa powder because I want to create the kind of divine, seductive, milky white chocolate taste that makes you think of snuggling down on a sheepskin rug in front of a roaring log fire. This recipe is quite a hit among children and a great one to whip up for kids' parties.

makes about 14 balls

300 ml oats
100 ml white sugar or icing sugar
15 ml vanilla sugar
100 ml vanilla powder
pinch of sea salt
30 ml organic salted butter
100 ml white chocolate chips
30 ml condensed milk or almond milk

garnish with… desiccated coconut
or crushed ground almonds

Melt the butter and white chocolate with the milk in a small saucepan over a low heat. Stir constantly with a wooden spoon so the milk doesn't curdle. Set aside to cool.

In a large bowl, mix the oats, sugar, vanilla sugar, vanilla powder, sea salt, and some of the crushed almonds.

Fold in the cooled butter, white chocolate and milk mixture. Mix well with your hands or a wooden spoon. If the mix becomes too wet, add more oats until it reaches the correct sticky texture and then place the bowl in the fridge for half an hour to set.

Using a tablespoon, take a scoop from the mix and place it in the palm of your hand. Form a ball and set aside on a tray or plate. Repeat.

Tip: These white chokladbollar tend to be dense and sweet, so I recommend rolling them a little smaller than usual.

Place your garnish of choice into a small bowl. Take a ball and drop it into the garnish, rolling it until coated.

Place balls onto a plate and leave in the fridge for at least an hour before serving.

fruit

an apple ball a day...

From American apple pie to *apfelstrudel*, apple cake to Dutch apple cake, everyone loves baking with apples. When I lived in New York City, there was a big farmers' market in Union Square I would frequent once a week to pick up fresh seasonal produce. The crisp smell of wet leaves and wet earth in the air made it my favorite time of year. American families would typically rake leaves or go apple picking in the nearest apple orchard. The ovens would fire up with butter, sugar, cinnamon and apples. There's something comforting about ordering a slice of apple pie.

makes about 14 small balls

300 ml oats
50 ml white sugar
15 ml vanilla sugar
30 ml apple juice
50 ml icing sugar
pinch of sea salt
40 g organic salted butter
100 ml white chocolate chips
50 ml crushed cinnamon cookies or ginger thins
1 apple
1 ml cinnamon powder
50 ml raw brown sugar

garnish with... icing sugar or crushed cookies or almonds

Melt half the butter and white chocolate in a small saucepan over a low heat. Set aside to cool.

In a large bowl, mix the oats, sugar, vanilla sugar, icing sugar, sea salt, and pinch of cinnamon. Mix well with a wooden spoon.

Add the apple juice to the dry ingredients and mix well with your hands.

Fold in the cooled butter and white chocolate mixture. Mix well with a wooden spoon then continue mixing with your hands, kneading the mixture gently. If the mix becomes too wet, add more oats until it reaches the correct sticky texture and then place the bowl in the fridge for half an hour to set.

apple filling

Peel and dice the apple into tiny cubes.

In a small saucepan, melt the remaining butter then add the diced apple over low heat. Add the raw brown sugar and cinnamon.

Reduce, so the apple is soft and slightly caramelized. Stir the mix frequently to make sure the apples don't burn. Cool.

Using a tablespoon, take a scoop from the mix and place in the palm of your hand. Form a ball and set aside on a tray or plate. Repeat.

Tip: These white chokladbollar tend to be dense and sweet, so I recommend rolling them a little smaller than usual.

Take each ball in your palm and with your thumb make an indentation in the middle of the ball. Put a small amount of apple mixture into each ball with the teaspoon. Fold, mold, reform, and roll the balls.

Place your garnish of choice into a small bowl. Take a ball and drop it into the garnish, rolling until coated.

blue balls: sesame blue

Sorry for the name… blueberries are a luxury in Southeast Asia because they're imported and expensive but they're a common sight in the Nordic countries. In Finland, blueberry juice is commonplace and Finnair serves blueberry juice on their regional European flights. Filled with antioxidants, blueberry is often used in smoothies, yogurts, teas, cakes, jams, and even skincare for its nutritional value. There are two variations to the blueberry chokladbollar. One involves blending a sesame and crushed blueberry filling into the mixture and the other one features carob and has a whole frozen blueberry stuffed inside.

makes about 12 medium-large balls

300 ml oats
100 ml raw brown sugar
15 ml vanilla sugar or vanilla essence
100 ml cocoa powder
25 g organic salted butter
pinch of sea salt
15 ml blueberry jam or homemade blueberry preserve
15 ml sesame seeds
100 ml dark chocolate chips
30 ml cold pressed coffee

garnish with… sesame seeds

Prepare your filtered cold pressed coffee the day before. If you have a French press, brew the coffee and let it sit in the French press for about 15 minutes before pressing down. Store the whole French press in the fridge overnight.

Melt the butter and chocolate in a small saucepan over a low heat. Set aside to cool.

In a large bowl, mix the oats, sugar, vanilla sugar, sea salt, sesame seeds, cocoa powder and blueberry jam. Mix well with a wooden spoon and use your hands to break up any clumps.

Slowly fold in half the melted butter and chocolate.
Mix well with your hands.

Add the cold pressed coffee and blueberry jam and mix thoroughly with your hands.

Using a tablespoon, take a scoop from the mix and place in the palm of your hand. Form a ball and set aside on a tray or plate. Repeat.

Dip the balls in the remaining butter and melted chocolate mixture until the entire ball is coated.
On a separate plate, roll the balls in the sesame until the entire ball is coated.

Store in the fridge for about an hour before serving.

make me blue-tiful antioxidant balls

Bitter. Dark. Antioxidant loaded. Healthy. Good for those who are health-conscious, vegan, and want an energetic boost at fika time.

makes about 12 medium-large balls

300 ml oats
100 ml raw brown sugar
15 ml vanilla sugar or vanilla essence
100 ml cocoa powder
25 g virgin coconut oil
pinch of sea salt
15 ml blueberry jam or homemade blueberry preserve
15 ml carob nibs
100 ml dark chocolate chips
30 ml cold pressed coffee
12 frozen blueberries

garnish with… melted dark chocolate, carob nibs, pearl sugar

Prepare your filtered cold pressed coffee the day before. If you have a French press, brew the coffee and let it sit in the French press for about 15 minutes before pressing down. Then store the whole French press in the fridge overnight.

Put the blueberries in the freezer while you make the mixture for the balls. When you are ready to stuff the balls with the blueberries, the cold blueberries will be less sticky than if you had used fresh blueberries.

Heat up the coconut oil and chocolate in a small saucepan over a low heat. Set aside to cool.

In a large bowl, mix the oats, sugar, vanilla sugar, sea salt, carob nibs, cocoa powder, and blueberry jam. Mix well with a wooden spoon, using your hands to break up any clumps.

Fold in half of the oil and melted chocolate slowly into the mixture. Mix well with your hands.

Add the cold pressed coffee and blueberry jam and mix thoroughly with your hands.

Using a tablespoon, take a scoop from the mix and place in the palm of your hand. Form and roll into balls. Place the balls on a plate or a tray. Repeat.

Take the blueberries out of the freezer.

Take each ball in your palm and with your thumb make an indentation in the middle of the ball. Slide a blueberry into the center of each ball. Fold, mold, reform, and roll the balls.

Dip each of the balls into the remaining coconut oil and melted chocolate mixture, coating each ball thoroughly with chocolate. Place the balls on a plate or tray.

Garnish the top of each ball with some carob nibs and pearl sugar.

Place the balls in the fridge for about an hour before serving.

monkey balls

When I lived in New York and the weather was less than ideal, we'd make chocolate banana bread. The fragrance of ooey-gooey chocolate, flour and banana would waft through the air. The inspiration to make a chokladbollar version of chocolate banana bread came to me during a rainy day in Singapore. The tropical storms would make everything dark, the winds would howl, and everything outside would be wet. My craving for banana and chocolate created this concoction. I hope you enjoy it!

makes about 12-14 balls

400 ml oats
100 ml cocoa powder
100 ml raw cane sugar
15 ml vanilla sugar or vanilla essence
pinch of sea salt
one ripe banana
30 ml coffee
50 g organic salted butter
100 ml dark chocolate chips
50g dark baking chocolate

garnish with… coconut flakes, sesame seeds, or cocoa powder

Brew a single shot of espresso and set aside to cool.

Mash the ripe banana until it has the consistency of apple sauce. You'll want to use a ripe banana to get more flavor.

In a large bowl, add the oats, cocoa powder, raw cane sugar, vanilla sugar or vanilla essence, and sea salt. Combine with your hands, making sure all ingredients are mixed well.

Melt the butter and dark chocolate together in a small saucepan.

Slowly add the coffee to the dry ingredients, mixing well with a wooden spoon.

Fold in half the melted butter and chocolate mixture. Set aside the other for the garnish. Mix with a wooden spoon and then switch to working by hand.

Tip: Do not burn your fingers! I pour in the melted butter and chocolate mixture very slowly with a tablespoon before I work it with my hands.

Place the bowl into the fridge for about half an hour to harden it up a little – the addition of the ripe banana makes it a bit too wet in more humid climates.

Using a tablespoon, take a scoop from the mix and place it in the palm of your hand.
Form a ball and set aside on a tray or plate. Repeat.

Place your garnish of choice into a small bowl and set aside.

Dip the balls in the remaining melted butter and chocolate mixture until coated all over.

Roll the balls in garnish and place on a plate.

Cool the balls in the freezer for at least an hour before serving.

razzle dazzle raspberry

The raspberry is such a fickle berry in warmer climates with a high humidity. It's so rare I get to indulge in raspberries but they go so perfectly with chocolate and are sweet but also a bit tart. They're wonderful in desserts and the juicy flesh can make a dark chocolate tart fresher and less dense or a fruit tart light and summery. I wanted these to look a little bit like the Nordic Christmas elves called *tomten*, which have a pointed top hat.

makes about 12 medium balls

300 ml oats
100 ml raw brown sugar
15 ml vanilla sugar
100 ml cocoa powder
25 g organic salted butter
pinch of sea salt
100 ml dark chocolate chips
24 raspberries
30 ml cold coffee

garnish with… melted dark chocolate, raspberry, and icing sugar

Place 12 raspberries in the freezer while you make the mixture for the balls. When you're ready to stuff the balls with the raspberries, the cold raspberries will be less sticky. The remaining 12 will go on top as a garnish so just keep them in the fridge.

Prepare the coffee and set aside to cool.

Melt the butter and chocolate in a small saucepan over a low heat. Set aside to cool.

In a large bowl, mix the oats, sugar, vanilla sugar, sea salt and cocoa powder. Mix well with a wooden spoon, using your hands to break up any clumps.

Add the cold coffee and mix well with your hands.

Fold in a little more than half of the melted butter and chocolate slowly into the mixture. Set aside the other half for the garnish. Mix well with your hands.

Using a tablespoon, take a scoop from the mix and place in the palm of your hand. Form and roll into balls and set aside on a plate or a tray. Repeat.

Take the raspberries out of the freezer.

Take a ball in the palm of your hand and with your thumb make an indentation in the middle of the ball. Slide a raspberry into the center of each ball. Fold, mold, reform, and roll the balls. Place each ball in a paper cupcake tin – this will contain any melted chocolate spillage.

Drizzle the remaining melted chocolate over the top of each ball. Delicately place a raspberry on top.

Store in the fridge for about an hour before serving.

Sprinkle a little icing sugar over the balls in front of your guests to mimic snow. The kids will love it!

strawberry fields of chocolate morsels

Summer is a time for berry picking and bubbly drinks on the patio. The image of Swedish strawberries always brings me back to the small Scandinavian studies department common room where we would have Ingmar Bergman film nights over some wine and beer. Black and white films with images of the Swedish countryside would dance across the TV. This recipe uses normal strawberries but you could easily use wild Swedish strawberries called *smultron*, which are much smaller and concentrated in flavor. I used regular strawberries, thinking also of the farmers' markets in New York City and buying baskets of strawberries to take for picnics in Central Park near the iconic Strawberry Fields.

makes about 12 medium-large balls

300 ml oats
100 ml raw brown sugar
15 ml vanilla bean powder
100 ml cocoa powder
pinch of sea salt
15 ml strawberry jam preserve
100 ml dark chocolate chips
25 g organic salted butter
30 ml lemon-verbena tea or chamomile tea
12 fresh strawberries (small)

garnish with… melted dark chocolate and dried strawberries, apple chips or pomegranate seeds

Put the strawberries in the freezer while you make the mixture for the balls. When you're ready to stuff the balls with the strawberries, the cold strawberries will be less sticky than if you had used fresh strawberries.

Prepare the tea and set aside to cool.

Melt the butter and chocolate in a small saucepan over a low heat. Set aside to cool.

In a large bowl, combine the oats, sugar, vanilla bean, sea salt, and cocoa powder. Mix well with a wooden spoon, using your hands to break up any clumps.

Slowly fold in half the melted butter and chocolate. Set aside the other half of the garnish.

Add the tea and strawberry jam preserve and mix thoroughly with your hands.

Using a tablespoon, take a scoop from the mix and place it in the palm of your hand. Form and roll into balls and set aside on a plate or tray. Repeat.

Take the strawberries out of the freezer.

Take each ball in your palm and with your thumb make an indentation in the middle of the ball. Slide a strawberry into the center of each ball. Fold, mold, reform, and roll the balls.

Dip each of the balls into the remaining melted butter and chocolate mixture, coating each ball thoroughly with chocolate. Place the balls onto a plate or tray.

Garnish the top of each ball with tiny pieces of the dried fruit of your choice.

Place the balls in the fridge for about an hour before serving.

vegan monkey balls

These balls are the vegan version of my banana chocolate monkey balls. Though similar in many ways, by substituting coconut oil for butter, the banana flavors come out more than in the regular version. It really surprised me how different chokladbollar can end up just by substituting and using different ingredients. The ripe banana and dark chocolate are the keys to making these balls taste more like a dense chocolate banana cake.

makes about 12-14 balls

400 ml oats
100 ml cocoa powder
100 ml raw brown sugar
1 ripe banana
50 g coconut oil
30 ml espresso coffee
15 ml vanilla sugar
pinch of sea salt
50 g dark baking chocolate

garnish with… melted dark chocolate, desiccated coconut flakes or pearl sugar

Prepare the espresso coffee and set aside to cool. Depending on your preference, start with a medium roast coffee bean or use a dark roast for a stronger coffee flavor. That said, in using an espresso the intensity of the coffee should come through either way.

Mash the ripe banana until it has the consistency of apple sauce. Make sure you use a ripe banana so you get all the yummy banana flavors shining through.

Place all dry ingredients in a large bowl and mix well.

Melt dark chocolate with coconut oil in the microwave for about a minute. Heating this in the microwave rather than in a saucepan ensures that the chocolate and coconut oil don't burn.

Add the coffee and mix well.

Fold in half the hot melted dark chocolate and coconut oil. Set aside the other half for the garnish.

Mix all ingredients thoroughly with your hands.

Place the bowl in the fridge for about half an hour to harden it up a little. The addition of the ripe banana can make it a bit too wet in more humid climates.

Fill a small bowl with coconut flakes.

Using a tablespoon, take a scoop from the mix and place in the palm of your hand. Form and roll into balls and set aside on a plate or a tray. Repeat.

Dip and roll the balls in the remaining melted dark chocolate and coconut oil mixture.

Place the balls in small cupcake paper cups and then drizzle a pinch of the coconut flakes over the balls.

Store the balls in the freezer for at least an hour before serving.

white lemon *dröm*

I grew up in hot climates and do not particularly like getting sticky, sweaty or sunburnt, which is probably why I like spending time indoors – where there's air conditioning, cold drinks, and I can choose when I want to be sweaty. Lemon bars, pavlova – a popular dessert consisting of fruit and meringue, lemon meringue pie, lemon curd and lemonade are all associated with that freshness and fruitiness I crave in the summer months. This recipe was created on a hot day in Malta in an effort to cool off. Though not as light as a lemon meringue pie, the citrus and light white chocolate are so complementary that this would be a great midsummer fika treat with a lemonade or iced tea.

makes about 12 balls

300 ml oats
100 ml white sugar or icing sugar
15 ml vanilla sugar
30 ml cold lemonade
30 ml organic salted butter
100 ml white chocolate
30 ml condensed milk or oat milk
30 ml lemon curd or jam
15 ml sesame seeds, crushed almonds, peanuts or hazelnuts (nuts optional)
pinch of sea salt

garnish with… melted white chocolate and sea salt, pearl sugar, candied fruit or ginger

Melt the butter and white chocolate in a small saucepan over a low heat. Stir constantly with a wooden spoon so the chocolate doesn't curdle. Set aside to cool.

In a large bowl, mix oats, sugar, vanilla sugar, sea salt, and nuts (optional). Slowly add the cold lemonade, condensed milk, and half the lemon curd, and mix well.

Place the rest of the lemon curd in the fridge to cool. This will make it easier to scoop and stuff into the center of your balls.

Fold in half the melted butter and white chocolate. Mix well with your hands. Set aside the other half of the melted butter and white chocolate mixture for the garnish.

If the mix becomes too wet, add more oats and make sure the oats are well mixed in with all the ingredients. Place the bowl in the fridge for half an hour to set.

Using a tablespoon, take a scoop from the mix and place in the palm of your hand. Form and roll into balls and set aside on a plate or a tray. Repeat.

Take the lemon curd out of the fridge and set it aside.

Place a ball in the palm of your hand and with your thumb, make a small indentation in the ball. Using a teaspoon, scoop a small amount of the lemon curd and stuff it into the center of the ball.

Fold the ends of the ball so the lemon curd is completely sealed in. Reform and roll the balls so they're spherical in shape. Repeat until all the balls are filled with lemon curd and neatly placed on your plate or tray.

Using a tablespoon, drizzle a bit of the remaining melted butter and white chocolate mixture on top of each ball.

Garnish the top of the white chocolate with sea salt, pearl sugar or candied fruit. Place the balls in the fridge for at least an hour before serving.

nut

almond loveballs

Almonds are probably my favorite nut because of their versatility, flavor, supposed health benefits, and because they can be savory or sweet. Raw, roasted, as marzipan or as almond butter, almonds are versatile. But my favorite is when they're paired with chocolate. This recipe is stuffed with small morsels of marzipan. I used to love eating marzipan chocolates as a kid – gorging on the sugary sweet flavor of the almonds. I had a favorite German bakery that we would frequent in Jakarta to get the best cakes and marzipan chocolates. It took years before I could eat marzipan again because it's often cloyingly sweet and overpowering and I had overdone it. In Brussels, marzipan chocolates were a popular treat during the Christmas season. I rediscovered marzipan after traveling to Copenhagen and Vienna where they emphasize more of the almond essence rather than just the sugar. I wanted to encapsulate the sweetness of marzipan with a mixture that marries it with the nutty and roasted flavors of almond in this recipe for a sweet and salty pairing. If you love almonds, this is the chokladbollar for you!

makes about 12-14 balls

300 ml oats
100 ml cocoa powder
100 ml raw brown sugar
25 g organic salted butter
1 tbsp almond butter
30 ml espresso coffee
1 vanilla pod
15 ml marzipan
pinch of sea salt

garnish with… crushed ground almonds, melted dark chocolate

Prepare the espresso and set aside to cool.

In a large bowl, mix the oats, cocoa powder, raw brown sugar, vanilla bean and sea salt.

Cut the vanilla pod vertically in half. Scrape out the vanilla bean into the dry ingredients and mix well.

Melt the butter and dark chocolate in a small saucepan and set aside to cool.

Add the coffee slowly to the dry ingredients and mix well.

Add the almond butter and mix well. Slowly pour half the melted butter and dark chocolate to the mixture.

Mix well with your hands until the consistency of the ingredients is sticky but not too wet.

Set aside in the fridge for about half an hour.

Using a tablespoon, take a scoop from the mix and place in the palm of your hand. Form and roll into balls and set aside on a plate or a tray. Repeat.

Using a teaspoon, scoop a small amount of marzipan and stuff it into the center of the ball and form.

Place your garnish of choice into a small bowl and set aside.

Dip the balls and roll them gently in the remaining melted butter and dark chocolate mixture until the whole ball is covered.

Take a ball and drop it into the garnish, rolling until coated.

all about almonds and hazelnuts

I love the taste of almonds and hazelnuts with chocolate. This recipe is my version of the Ferrero Rocher. As a child, I used to love getting those gold wrapped chocolates at Christmas time, opening them, and sticking the whole thing in my mouth. The nutty chocolate morsels were truly the perfect mix of crunch, chocolate, creaminess, and sugar. Instead of using vanilla essence or vanilla sugar, this recipe uses real vanilla bean.

makes about 12-14 balls

300 ml oats
100 ml cocoa powder
100 ml raw cane sugar
pinch of sea salt
1 vanilla pod
30 ml coffee
30 g organic salted butter
1 tbsp chocolate hazelnut spread or almond butter
30 g dark baking chocolate

garnish with… chopped almonds or hazelnuts

Brew a single shot of espresso and set aside to cool.

In a large bowl, add the oats, cocoa powder, raw cane sugar, and sea salt. Combine with your hands, making sure all the ingredients are mixed well.

Cut the vanilla pod vertically in half and dig out the tiny seeds. Put directly in the bowl and mix in with your hands.

In a small saucepan, melt the butter until slightly browned then add the chocolate to the pan. Stir constantly so the chocolate melts but does not burn like the butter.

Slowly add the espresso to the dry ingredients, mixing well with a wooden spoon.

Fold in half the melted butter and chocolate mixture to the dry ingredients. Mix with a wooden spoon and then switch to working by hand.

Tip: Don't burn your fingers! I pour in the melted butter and chocolate mixture very slowly with a tablespoon before I work it with my hands.

Using a tablespoon, take a scoop from the mix and place in the palm of your hand. Form and roll into balls and set aside on a plate or a tray. Repeat.

Place your garnish of choice into a small bowl and set aside.

Dip the balls into the remaining melted butter and chocolate mixture until coated all over.

Roll the balls in the garnish and place on a plate.

Cool the balls in the fridge for at least one hour before serving.

gimme my nutty balls: peanut butter and chocolate

This recipe is inspired by the American chocolate Reese's pieces peanut butter cups with their combination of chocolate and peanut butter. I remember that first bite – milky chocolate with a thick peanut butter sugar bomb center. Someone had brought the candy from the US base shop for the whole class. Growing up at international schools, I was exposed to American, British, Australian and other candies from all over the world that friends brought in for birthday parties, celebrations, and after school events. Reese's pieces is a common American candy that children love, and the salty sweet explosion delighted me as a preteen with a sweet tooth.

makes about 12-14 balls

400 ml oats
100 ml cocoa powder
100 ml raw brown sugar
50 g organic salted butter
100 ml dark chocolate chips (70%)
30 ml coffee or English breakfast tea
1 tbsp organic peanut butter
15 ml vanilla sugar or vanilla essence
pinch of sea salt

garnish with… melted dark chocolate and hazelnuts

Melt the butter and dark chocolate in a saucepan on low heat, taking extra care not to burn the chocolate. An alternative is to melt the chocolate with the butter in microwave.

Place all dry ingredients in a large bowl and mix well.

Add the vanilla sugar or vanilla essence to the dry ingredients and mix.

Add the coffee or tea and mix well.

Fold in a third of the hot melted butter and dark chocolate. Add the peanut butter to the mix. Set aside the rest of the butter and chocolate for dipping.

Mix all ingredients thoroughly.

Using a tablespoon, take a scoop from the mix and place it in the palm of your hand. Form a ball and set aside on a tray or plate. Repeat.

Drop the balls in the remaining melted chocolate and butter mixture. Place each ball in the cupcake cups.

Tip: This could get messy! Cupcake paper cups keep the melted chocolate contained.

Sprinkle with hazelnuts.

Store the balls in the freezer for at least an hour before serving.

pistache

Pistachio gelato is one of my favorite flavors. I wanted to recreate the sweet refreshing nutty taste of pistachio ice cream in this chokladbollar. Pistachio's such a versatile nut and can taste salty or sweet. I once attended a chocolate tasting event at the Chocolate Company in Rotterdam where they had a pistachio jam spread that smelled amazing. I knew I had to utilize this in a pistachio flavored *chokladboll*.

makes about 12 small balls

300 ml oats
50 ml raw brown sugar
15 ml vanilla essence
100 ml cocoa powder
pinch of sea salt
30 g pistachio jam[1]
100 ml dark chocolate chips
30 ml cold black coffee

garnish with… melted dark chocolate, crushed pistachio, desiccated coconut, pearl sugar

In a large bowl, mix the oats, sugar, vanilla essence, cocoa powder and sea salt.

Melt the chocolate chips in a small bowl in the microwave for about 45 seconds to a minute. Stir the chips and set aside.

Add the cold black coffee to the dry ingredients. Mix well with your hands.

Add in half the melted chocolate and mix again with your hands, kneading the mixture until it reaches a sticky consistency and is ready for forming and rolling into balls.

Using a tablespoon, take a scoop of the mix and place it in the palm of your hand. Form and roll into balls and set aside on a plate or a tray. Repeat.

Take each ball in your palm and with your thumb make an indentation in the middle of the ball. Insert a small amount of pistachio jam into the center of each ball, using a teaspoon. Fold, mold, reform, and roll the balls.

Dip and roll the balls in the remaining melted chocolate until fully coated.

Place the balls in paper cupcake tins and drizzle your of choice toppings over the top.

Store the balls in fridge for about an hour before serving.

---

[1] *If you can't find this, grind pistachio very finely with a spoonful of butter and a spoonful of white sugar to use as an alternative.*

holiday

candy cane
jultidschokladbollar

I love candy canes and every holiday season when they show up in the stores, there's always a box of these peppermint canes of sugar. Mint and chocolate are probably my favorite combination. There's something about the freshness of the mint and the creaminess of chocolate that's soothing. The fun involved in adding crushed candy canes on desserts during the holiday season can help one get into the mood of getting cozy with blankets, a hot beverage, and snuggling by the fireplace with loved ones.

makes about 14 small balls

300 ml oats
100 ml raw brown sugar
15 ml vanilla sugar
15 ml crushed candy cane
100 ml cocoa powder or peppermint cocoa powder
pinch of sea salt
30 g organic salted butter
100 ml dark chocolate
30 ml cold coffee infused with a candy cane

garnish with… crushed candy cane

Prepare your coffee and while it's still hot, drop a candy cane into the mug to melt and infuse in the coffee while it cools.

Melt the butter and chocolate in a small saucepan over a low heat and set aside.

In a large bowl, mix the oats, sugar, vanilla sugar, cocoa powder, sea salt, and crushed candy cane. Mix all ingredients well.

Pour the candy cane infused cold coffee into the mixture.

Fold in the melted butter and chocolate and blend well with a wooden spoon.

Using your hands, mix all ingredients thoroughly and knead until the contents are combined. Place in the fridge for about 20 minutes if the mixture is still a bit sticky.

Using a tablespoon, take a scoop of the mix and place it in the palm of your hand. Form and roll into balls and set aside on a plate or a tray. Repeat.

On a plate, place the crushed candy cane topping.

Tip: Crush the candy canes in a Ziploc bag with a rolling pin. The candy cane does not have to be finely ground. You will want small enough pieces that will still give a crunch.

Take a ball and drop it in the crushed candy canes, rolling until coated.

Place the balls in the fridge for about an hour before serving.

chocolate salty caramel balls

Yes, I know about the chocolate salty balls song… chocolate and salt is a combination particularly loved by women. Salted caramel had a bit of a moment a couple of years ago and in the US, caramels are still a popular Christmas gift. You can find salted caramel everything – from ice cream to cupcakes. I like the combination of cloyingly sweet caramel and a punch of sea salt in the sauce. The idea is to have a sweet salty surprise in the center that comes oozing out. It's a favorite among my friends and they request it a bit too much!

makes about 12 balls

300 ml oats
100 ml raw brown sugar
15 ml vanilla bean powder
100 ml cocoa powder
2 pinches of sea salt
30 g organic salted butter
30 ml cold coffee
50 ml dark chocolate chips
30 ml salted caramel sauce[1]

garnish with… chocolate sprinkles and sea salt

---

[1] Salted caramel sauce is available at many quality grocers in the jam section.

Prepare your coffee beforehand and set aside to cool.

Place the caramel sauce in the fridge until you're ready to stuff the balls.

Melt the butter in a saucepan until slightly browned and burnt; set aside.

Melt the dark chocolate chips in the melted butter or separately, in the microwave.

In a large bowl, mix the oats, sugar, vanilla sugar, cocoa powder, and sea salt with your hands, making sure there are no clumps in the dry ingredients.

Add the cold coffee to the mixture and mix well.

Slowly fold the butter into the dry ingredients. Use a wooden spoon to mix the ingredients until cool enough to use your hands. Knead until thoroughly mixed and slightly sticky.

Take the caramel out of the fridge.

Using a tablespoon, take a scoop of the mix and place it in the palm of your hand. Form and roll into balls and set aside on a plate or a tray. Repeat.

Pour some chocolate sprinkles on a plate, ready for rolling the balls in.

Take each ball in your palm and with your thumb, make an indentation in the middle of the ball. Place a small amount of the caramel into each ball using the teaspoon. Fold, mold, reform, and roll the balls.

Roll the balls over the chocolate sprinkles. Repeat.

Place each ball in individual cupcake paper cups and lightly sprinkle sea salt over the top of each ball.

Place the balls in the fridge for about an hour before serving.

fudgy chocolate

Fudge. I used to make homemade fudge as a Christmas gift for my friends when I lived in New York. There's something so indulgent yet personal about giving homemade gifts. I made regular chocolate fudge and peppermint chocolate fudge. When you bite into the smooth fudge there's this gooey milky texture and sweetness that's just so nice in winter. In Sweden, they have candy called *kola* which is something in between caramel and fudge. This seems to be the candy Swedes make during the holiday season. I like good old-fashioned American fudge for that double whammy of chocolate. If you're feeling a little too lazy to make your own fudge, you can always just buy Daim chocolate brittle or toffee to stuff the chokladbollar.

makes about 12-14 balls

300 ml oats
100 ml cocoa powder
100 ml raw brown sugar
30 g organic salted butter
30 ml cold coffee
15 ml vanilla sugar
1 tbsp chocolate spread or melted dark chocolate
pinch of sea salt
12-14 small cubes of fudge candy, prepared or bought the day before

garnished with… desiccated coconut, pearl sugar or crushed candy canes

Place all dry ingredients in a large bowl and mix well.

Melt the butter in a saucepan until slightly browned.

Add the coffee and mix well.

Fold in the hot melted butter. If the mixture seems a bit too wet, you can add more oats.

Mix all ingredients thoroughly with your hands.

Chill the mixture in the fridge for about 30 minutes.

Using a tablespoon, take a scoop from the mix and place in the palm of your hand. Form and roll into balls and set aside on a plate or a tray. Repeat.

Put a ball in your palm and with your thumb make an indentation in the middle of the ball. Slide a small piece of fudge candy into the center of each ball. Fold, mold, reform, and roll the balls.

Place your garnish of choice into a small bowl. Take a ball and drop it into the garnish, rolling until coated.

Store the balls in the freezer for at least an hour before serving.

»

good old-fashioned fudge

makes one tray of fudge

30 g salted organic butter
pinch of sea salt
30 ml condensed milk or maple syrup (for vegan version)
150 ml milk or dark chocolate chips
15 ml raw brown sugar
5 ml cocoa powder

In a saucepan, heat the butter over medium heat until melted.

Add the chocolate chips and stir constantly over low heat.

Pour in condensed milk and stir constantly over low heat.

Add the brown sugar, sea salt, and cocoa powder. Mix well, then turn off heat.

Pour the liquid over a small tray and store overnight in the freezer.

Take out the next day and let it defrost before cutting into 12 small cubes.

world

earl grey

My favorite tea is Earl Grey. There's a specialty tea shop in Singapore called TWG that has a delectable selection of teas and tea-infused French macarons. My favorite is their Earl Grey chocolate macaron. I wanted to make Earl Grey-infused chokladbollar that evoke a similar delicate flavor without overpowering the chocolate.

makes about 12-14 balls

300 ml oats
100 ml cocoa powder
100 ml raw brown sugar
30 g organic salted butter
40 ml cold Earl Grey tea
15 ml vanilla sugar
3 tbsp melted dark chocolate
pinch of sea salt

garnish with… Earl Grey-infused melted dark chocolate and your choice of toppings, for example: crunchy chocolate, marshmallows, pearl sugar, candied fruit, edible flower petals, herbs, coconut or nuts

Prepare your Earl Grey tea ahead of time so it's really dark and strong.

Melt the butter with chocolate in a saucepan over a low heat and add about 20 ml of Earl Grey to the mixture.

Place the oats, cocoa powder, raw brown sugar, and vanilla sugar in a large bowl and mix well.

Add the remainder of the Earl Grey to the dry ingredients and mix well.

Slowly fold in half the melted butter and chocolate. Mix well with your hands. If the mixture seems a bit too wet, add more oats.

Mix all ingredients thoroughly with your hands.

Using a tablespoon, take a scoop of the mix and place it in the palm of your hand. Form and roll into balls and set aside on a plate or a tray. Repeat.

Dip and coat each ball in the remaining melted butter and chocolate until fully covered. Place each ball in a paper cupcake tin to contain the chocolate.

Drizzle your chosen toppings over the top of the chokladbollar.

Store the balls in the freezer for at least an hour before serving.

kokos kokos coconuts *kaya*

dairy-free

Kaya is a sweet coconut jam common in Singapore and Malaysia. Usually eaten with buttered toast for breakfast or a mid-afternoon snack, it's the Southeast Asian equivalent of a fika treat. Made with eggs, sugar, coconut milk, and sometimes pandan leaves, kaya is dairy-free and perfect for those with lactose allergies. I always experiment with local ingredients in making chokladbollar wherever my travels take me. In Singapore, you can find local coffeeshops serving kaya toast and grocery stores with kaya jams so it's fitting to swap butter for this sweet coconut jam. Because the jam is already sweet, feel free to use less sugar for this recipe. I've added a recipe for kaya jam that is also easy but takes a bit of time to make so it is recommended to make the kaya jam a day before.

makes about 12 small balls

300 ml oats
50 ml raw brown sugar
15 ml vanilla essence
100 ml cocoa powder
pinch of sea salt
30 g kaya jam
100 ml dark chocolate chips
30 ml cold black coffee

garnish with… desiccated coconut or pearl sugar

In a large bowl, mix the oats, sugar, vanilla essence, cocoa powder, and sea salt and mix well.

Melt the chocolate chips in a small bowl in the microwave for about 45 seconds to a minute. Stir the chips and set aside.

Add the cold black coffee to the dry ingredients.
Mix well with your hands.

Add the kaya jam and melted chocolate and mix well with your hands, kneading the mixture until sticky and ready for forming and rolling into balls.

Using a tablespoon, take a scoop of the mix and place it in the palm of your hand. Form and roll into balls and set aside on a plate or a tray. Repeat.

Place your garnish of choice into a small bowl. Take a ball and drop it into the garnish, rolling until coated.

Store the balls in the fridge for about an hour before serving.

kaya jam

3 eggs
225 g sugar
350 ml coconut milk
2-3 pandan leaves or bay leaves

In a bowl, combine coconut milk and 100 g of sugar. Whisk the sugar until dissolved.

Add eggs and whisk everything well.

In a small saucepan, melt the rest of the sugar over medium heat. The sugar will clump and then become a thick syrup as it browns and caramelizes. Once the syrup is the color of brown caramel, turn off the heat. Do not overcook as the syrup can burn.

Slowly fold the caramel syrup into the coconut milk and egg mixture, whisking as you do so. The syrup will harden a little as it mixes in. Continue to whisk and break up the clumps.

Fill a small saucepan about a third with water and heat it to a gentle simmer over a low heat.

Place the mixing bowl over the saucepan, the base of the mixing bowl above water level. Add the knotted pandan or bay leaves.

Gently cook the mixture, stirring continually around the sides and the bottom of the mixing bowl. Remove the leaves once they turn pale and discard.

Continue to cook the mixture until it thickens to the desired consistency. This can take 45 minutes to an hour. Ideal consistency is when it's thick and coats your spoon like butter.

Remove from the heat and set aside to cool to room temperature. Store in an airtight container and refrigerate. It will keep for about two weeks, if stored in the fridge.

s'mores chokladbollar

The first time I had proper s'mores was in the forest at Lake Arrowhead, California during a summer figure skating camp. We spent all day training at the ice rink, ballet studio and gym. By the end of the week, we were tired and very hungry. The camp counselors arranged a bonfire at one of the campsites and we roasted marshmallows on sticks we had foraged in the forest. The marshmallow was placed between two Graham Crackers, along with a piece of chocolate that melted on contact with the hot marshmallow. The taste of the burnt, toasted, and caramelized marshmallow lingered on my tongue and the melted chocolate coated my fingers. I've since thought about how children in Sweden learn how to make chokladbollar and eat them after school as a commonplace fika treat and how it's not all that dissimilar from how children in America eat s'mores as an after school treat.

makes about 12-14 balls

300 ml oats
100 ml cocoa powder
100 ml raw brown sugar
30 ml espresso coffee
15 ml vanilla sugar
100 ml mini marshmallows
25 g dark chocolate
30 g butter
12-14 Graham Crackers or Ginger Thins
pinch of sea salt

garnish with… melted dark chocolate, desiccated coconut flakes, or sea salt

Prepare your espresso coffee either with a coffee machine or moka pot and set aside to cool. You don't want to pour hot coffee over your dry ingredients because the mixture will be too wet.

Place your oats, brown sugar, vanilla sugar, cocoa powder, and sea salt in a large bowl and mix well with a wooden spoon, using your hands so that all the ingredients are thoroughly blended.

In a saucepan, melt the butter until slightly browned. The browned butter will add a caramel taste to the cocoa powder. Turn off the heat and melt the dark chocolate in the hot butter. Set aside to cool slightly.

In a separate saucepan, toast the mini marshmallows over a low heat. Make sure to turn them frequently so they don't stick to the pan. Once the marshmallows are slightly toasted, set them aside in a small bowl.

Slowly add the cooled coffee to the dry ingredients and mix well. Slowly fold in about half the butter and chocolate mixture to the dry ingredients. Mix with a wooden spoon, then continue mixing and kneading the ingredients with your hands until sticky.

Using a tablespoon, take a scoop of the mix and place it in the palm of your hand. Form and roll into balls and set aside on a plate or a tray. Repeat.

For each ball, make a small indentation in its center and stuff two to three mini marshmallows inside. Conceal the marshmallows as best you can, mold and reform the balls, and then dip them in the remaining melted chocolate and butter.

Place each ball on a cookie and sprinkle some desiccated coconut flakes and sea salt on top of each ball.

Chill the balls in the fridge for about an hour before serving.

swedish *kanelbullebollar* cinnamon balls

One of my favorite fika treats is *kanelbulle*, a Swedish cinnamon bun filled with a hint of cardamom and topped with pearl sugar. Most traditional cafés have kanelbulle. When paired with filtered black coffee for fika, these buns are very filling. I like to share a kanelbulle with a friend; the combination of cinnamon and cardamom reminds me of comfortable Christmas warmth. This recipe also utilizes crushed *pepparkakor*, the Swedish thin cinnamon cookies you can buy in IKEA around Christmas. Alternatively, Ginger Thins would work.

makes about 12 balls

200 ml oats
100 ml crushed pepparkakor cookies or Ginger Thins
30 g butter
15 ml cinnamon
5 ml cardamom
30 ml cold espresso coffee or regular black coffee
100 ml cocoa powder
100 ml raw brown sugar
1 scraped vanilla bean stalk or 5 ml vanilla bean powder
pinch of sea salt

garnish with... melted dark chocolate and crushed pepparkakor or Ginger Thins

Prepare an espresso or regular black coffee and set aside to cool.

Put the pepparkakor or Ginger Thins in a Ziploc bag and smash them until the cookies are ground to a fine powder. This can also be done in a food processor.

Melt the butter in the microwave or in a saucepan. Alternatively, the butter and dark chocolate can be melted together. Set aside to cool for a bit.

Place the oats, crushed cookies, vanilla, brown sugar, cinnamon, cardamom, sea salt and cocoa powder in a large bowl. Mix well with your hands. Add the cold espresso coffee in the dry ingredients and mix well.

Slowly fold in half of the melted butter and chocolate (if you prefer) into the bowl and mix well with a wooden spoon, before finishing off by mixing and kneading the mixture with your hands.

Set aside while you place the remaining melted butter and dark chocolate mix in a small bowl and a few extra crushed pepparkakor cookies on a separate plate. The crushed cookies for the topping do not need to be as finely ground as those used in the mix and can be crushed by hand.

Using a tablespoon, take a scoop of the mix and place it in the palm of your hand. Form and roll into balls and set aside on a plate or a tray. Repeat.

Dip the balls in the melted butter and chocolate, then roll the balls in the crushed pepparkakor.

As an additional garnish, you can also crush toffee or Daim chocolate together with pepparkakor for added crunch and flavor.

Place the balls in the fridge for about an hour before serving.

zen tea ceremony with matcha

Matcha is a potent green tea powder usually served at Japanese tea ceremonies. Each ceremony is served by the host like a slow dance ritual: delicate, precise, sophisticated and quiet. The first time I experienced a traditional Japanese tea ceremony was in middle school on a school exchange. I was studying Japanese at the time and we spent the whole day at the Japanese school learning about the school curriculum and culture. At the end of the day, the Japanese tea ceremony club entertained us with a whole ceremony. I loved how delicate the flavors of the tea became with the milky frothy texture from the whisking. Fika is taking time out of your day to recharge and a Japanese tea ceremony is likewise an honorable ritual, performed by the host for a guest, that slows down the pace of the outside world. A little bit of matcha powder goes a long way.

makes about 12-14 balls

300 ml oats
100 ml cocoa powder
100 ml raw brown sugar
30 g organic salted butter
50 ml matcha tea (pinch of matcha already whisked and blended with water)
15 ml vanilla sugar
100 ml melted dark chocolate (3 tbsp melted dark chocolate for the mixture)
pinch of sea salt

garnished with… melted dark, milk, or white chocolate, with a dusting of cocoa or matcha powder

Prepare your matcha tea ahead of time. In a small bowl, add a pinch of matcha powder to a small amount of water. Rapidly but carefully whisk the powder and water until frothy, then continue adding water until the desired concentration of tea is reached.

Melt the butter and chocolate in a saucepan over a low heat, adding about 20 ml of matcha tea to the mixture.

Place the oats, cocoa powder, raw brown sugar, and vanilla sugar in a large bowl and mix well.

Add the remainder of the matcha tea to the dry ingredients and mix well.

Fold in half the melted butter and chocolate slowly into the mixture. Mix well with your hands. If the mixture seems a bit too wet, add more oats.

Mix all the ingredients thoroughly with your hands.

Using a tablespoon, take a scoop of the mix and place it in the palm of your hand. Form and roll into balls and set aside on a plate or a tray. Repeat.

Dip and coat each ball in the rest of the melted butter and chocolate until fully covered. Place each ball in a paper cupcake case to contain the chocolate.

Drizzle the cocoa powder or a tiny bit of matcha powder over the top of the chokladbollar.

Store the balls in the freezer for at least an hour before serving.

profiles

stockholm

Dubbed 'the capital of Scandinavia' and the 'Venice of the North', Stockholmers are proud to call their city home. The capital of Sweden is teeming with life, and the bustle of trendy Stockholmers rushing through the architecturally impressive T-Banan metro stations is indicative of this exciting place. Despite the fast pace, Stockholm offers the visitor a plethora of historic architecture, royal palaces, trendy restaurants and bars, countless museums, islands, and the charming Gamla Stan (Old Town).

Winter, spring, summer or fall, this city has a lot to offer visitors, and the vibe changes totally depending on the season. From Christmas markets and candlelit dinners in winter, to cherry blossom viewing in the Kungsträdgården park in spring, island hopping in the summer, before snuggling up in the fall at one of the many cafés for an afternoon fika, I'm sure you'll be as enamored as I am with this stunning city.

Visit Stockholm's website is crammed with a variety of guides to get you started on your own love affair with the capital city or *huvudstad*.

Here's a list of the top ten attractions in Stockholm, according to Visit Stockholm:

- Vasa Museum
- The Royal Palace
- Fotografiska Museum
- Moderna Museum
- City Hall
- ABBA, the Museum
- Gamla Stan
- Skansen open air museum
- Gröna Lund amusement park
- Drottningholm Palace

www.visitstockholm.com

gast

Gast Café is tucked away on a small side street. I stumbled upon it one rainy Monday morning, on my way to meet Cymon Reid, operations manager for the Gast, Kaffeverket, and Snickarbacken cafés. With frazzled hair and damp socks, I stumbled into the warmth and candlelight. Diners were all comfortably busy sipping their lattés and cappuccinos while clacking away on computers or reading the morning paper.

Gast means 'ghost' in Swedish and the name is a nod to the Spökparken or 'spooky park' across the street. Schleffer Palace lies within the park, the site of much speculation and stories of ghost sightings. Gast Café has a cute ghost icon hanging above its guests that resembles more the ghost from Pac-Man than the lifelike sightings from across the street.

A steady stream of visitors passes through its doors as we sit at a candlelit round table for breakfast at the front of the minimalist space. Cymon mentions that the bulk of the clientele at the café comes from the nearby offices on the busy Sveavägen street. Gast Café's menu is in English, located as it is in the middle of central Stockholm, with global offices and boutique hotels nearby. About half of the people in there that day weren't Swedish.

Cymon isn't Swedish either but has called Stockholm home for the past decade. A Kiwi transplant, he started working in cafes in London and ended up running a small chain of cafés with his Swedish business partners in Stockholm. The opening of Gast is his latest project, and he explains that they wanted a place for people to have a great cup of coffee, complete with a menu of healthy and simple meals, and a traditional Swedish pastry selection, for fika purists.

www.gastcafe.se

kaffeverket

After a morning at Gast, Cymon, its operations manager and I braved the cold damp winter morning to have lunch at Kaffeverket, another of his enterprises, in the Vasastan district. A neighborhood café with specialty coffee and regular customers stopping by for a delicious salad bowl or sandwich, I realized how cozy Stockholm really can be during the dark winter months.

Stockholmers need places like Kaffeverket to duck into for fika when it's cold out. And with white brick walls, black and white photographs, wooden communal tables, candles, chatty baristas, and a wide variety of pastries at the counter, Kaffeverket is just the place.

Cymon explained that, upon opening in 2008, Kaffeverket was the first café to serve specialty coffee in the area. The residents of Vasastan were a little hesitant at first to try a new place, being creatures of habit and against paying extra for a supposedly better cup of specialty roast without the usual *påtår* (or second, free helping of coffee that one can commonly ask for in Sweden). Slowly, over time, locals realized that the coffee served was indeed better, however, and it had a sophisticated palate. They kept coming back. A steady stream of regulars from the area now pass through Kaffeverket's glass doors, and customers know the baristas behind the counter by name.

I was caught off guard by how friendly and warm the baristas were at engaging in conversation. Kaffeverket defies the reputation that service can be a little cold in Stockholm. Perhaps it was the chatty Australian barista, or the long communal tables, but this place could easily be described as *mysigt*, a Swedish word used to describe that familiar, warm sensation one gets from feeling comfortable in a particular setting.

www.kaffeverket.nu

snickarbacken

Once upon a time, I found a café that was artistic, cozy, quiet, and served a great cup of coffee and kanelbulle. I came back to search for that place so a friend who was visiting could experience a proper Swedish fika in a place that embodied trendy Stockholm and yet was comfortable enough for us to enjoy a good, long conversation. Snickarbacken was that place. After my rediscovery, it became one of my go-to spots for a leisurely fika in Stockholm.

Fast forward to a rainy winter's day café-hopping with Cymon, also the operations manager of Snickarbacken, as we arrived at our last stop for the day. The rain was pelting it down again and so it was nice to be able to escape into the cave-like, labyrinthine Snickarbacken, situated on a quiet street in the upscale Östermalm district. One of my favorite features of this café is the rotating gallery of artwork on its stark white walls. Provocative, interesting, quirky, and at times absurd, the art display changes frequently.

The menu offerings at Snickarbacken are similar to at Gast and Kaffeverket, but here the pastries and the coffee are the focus. Snickarbacken 7 is a place for a good old fika with friends. With so many tables, and a lifestyle concept store within the café, this place is a trendsetter. Digital nomads, trendy types, hipsters, students, and tourists abound and descend upon this busy yet cozy spot.

Cymon told me how he started working to transform Snickarbacken into one of the hottest spots for fika in Stockholm. Cymon and his team found this hidden, open space that felt transformative and calm, and with something regal about its high ceilings. They wanted to make this space a lifestyle concept café in which people could hang out by themselves, with friends, or perhaps on a fika date.

www.snickarbacken7.se

gothenburg

Gothenburgers are the friendliest Swedes you'll ever meet. They're known for being fun-loving, chatty, and laid-back. Their city is the second most populous in Sweden and has the freshest seafood you can find for miles. The city especially comes alive during the summer months when residents flock to its neighboring islands for some sun, sea, schnapps, and seafood – and fika by the water, of course!

Gothenburg, or Göteborg, has a rich maritime history dating back to the 1600s, when it was a trading colony, primarily inhabited by the Dutch. You can see the Dutch influence in the multitude of canals running through the city center.

One of my favorite memories of visiting Gothenburg is of having spent a warm summer's day on the island of Brännö, just south of the city limits, and drinking a light, fruity cider by the sea there. Trams run frequently throughout Gothenburg, so you can catch the never ending summer sun on the coast, or on an island, and then return to one of the lively bars in the center as dusk falls. The warm vibe of Gothenburg and its residents is sure to keep you charmed with laughter and adventure through the coldest winter nights, and beyond.

www.goteborg.com is the city's official tourism site and offers interesting titbits of information on the city.

Ten must-dos in Gothenburg, according to Goteborg.com:

- Have fun at Liseberg, Scandinavia's largest amusement park
- Visit the splendid Gothenburg Museum of Art
- Take a day trip to the Gothenburg archipelago
- Take a waterside city tour on the Paddan boat
- Buy seafood at Feskekôrka fish market
- Take a 'fika break' in Haga
- Go on safari through the rainforest at Universeum
- Shop for Gothenburg designs
- Indulge in seafood
- Visit the Garden Society in the city center

www.goteborg.com

brogyllen

Wherever I am in the world, it's always fun to go to traditional bakeries. So, when I received the email invitation to visit the Brogyllen *konditori* in Gothenburg, I was pretty excited. The Swedish konditori is a combined bakery and café that also serves breakfast, sandwiches and salads, and is a place for people to meet for fika with their friends and family. The focus of a konditori is the baked goods, of course, as well as the ambience.

Brogyllen is an institution within Gothenburg's fika scene. It has been well known ever since its humble beginnings as a bakery just outside of Gothenburg, in Landala. Brogyllen now has several locations in and around Gothenburg, and I visited the centrally-located outlet on Västra Hamngatan. Walking into the super crowded konditori with people of all ages, I felt a bit overwhelmed. This was a popular place! I was early for my meeting and peered over the counter to see numerous traditional Swedish delicacies: green princess cakes, cinnamon buns, and rows of *semla*. It was the time of year when Swedes eat copious amounts of these cream buns for the upcoming *fettisdagen* (Fat Tuesday).

I met with brand manager, Mimmi, who usually works at the Saluhallen location. She said, "Brogyllen has been making bread and pastries the same way since the very beginning." Many of the older Swedes who come to Brogyllen are traditionalists in the way they have their fika. Mimmi went on to say that, as a company, Brogyllen strives to honor the past but still wants to innovate in the way it presents items and develops recipes. This is no easy task while still keeping a reputation intact.

www.brogyllen.se (available only in Swedish)

da matteo

On a cold winter's day in Gothenburg, I was in search of a good cup of coffee from a local coffee roaster and stumbled upon da Matteo. Located in a trendy shopping district, da Matteo is the kind of place where you can sit for hours with a friend, or come in alone for coffee and a cinnamon bun, and never feel awkward or unwelcome. The vibe at da Matteo is chilled but not pretentious, cozy but not nap-inducing. I comfortably tucked into my coffee and chokladbollar while people-watching trendy hipsters – lattè mammas and lattè pappas having their afternoon fika with children and friends.

Operating in several locations within a few blocks of each other, da Matteo has become synonymous with Gothenburg's fika scene. From coffee roasting to cakes, cookies, tarts and breads, da Matteo make everything in-house, and their most popular fika treat is the kanelbulle.

The name itself comes from the founder's intention to blend Italian and Nordic cultures. By paying more attention to coffee roasts, as the Italians do, the team at da Matteo is interested in enhancing the Swedish palate. Founder Matts Johansson says that the typical flavor profile of coffee in Sweden tends to be full-bodied rather than the lighter, more delicate roasts found elsewhere – something he's eager to change.

Johansson explains, "Through further expansion and by introducing more customers to the great tastes of coffee and bread, we want to continue to play an important role in the Swedish coffee, bread and café markets."

www.damatteo.se

alkemisten kaffebar

I visited Alkemisten Kaffebar after a quick tram ride to the district neighborhood of Kvillebäcken, just outside central Gothenburg. Located on a small street corner just a couple of blocks from a local food market, the small café with colorful décor felt warm and welcoming. Alkemisten's concept is to serve organic coffee from local roasters and ethically-sourced homemade vegan food and pastries in a relaxed environment. I met with the sweet and softly-spoken vegan pastry chef, Felicia Gullstrand, to talk about fika and chokladbollar.

A self-taught, passionate vegan pastry chef, Felicia has been baking and making pastries since she was a child. We laughed and discussed the crazy recipes we both dream about in the small hours. I really admired her trailblazing, creative mindset and experimentation in the kitchen. She dreamt up all the recipes for the different types of *rawbollar* herself, with flavors like mango, green tea, mint, tahini, and lemon. It was so hard to decide which to choose! I ordered them all.

The people walking through Alkemisten's doors for afternoon fika linger for at least a couple of hours despite the limited seating. With the friendly baristas and colorful, quirky décor, one gets the feeling of being in the living room of a global traveler, and I immediately felt at home in the space. The hours flew by until I realized that Felicia and I had spent the entire afternoon talking, and it was now closing time.

www.alkemistenkaffebar.se

helsingborg

A picturesque city in Scania, or Skåne, the southernmost province of Sweden, Helsingborg is steeped in the history of Sweden's relationship with the Kingdom of Denmark. The city is located right by the Øresund strait where ferries to and from the small Danish city of Helsingør (aka Elsinore) showcase the continuing ties with the Danes.

Upon arriving at Helsingborg Central Station, the grand architecture of the majestic city hall, the Rådhuset, welcomes you with its mighty regalia. Walking further into the city center, you're greeted by the tall Kärnan tower overlooking the skyline.

Often overlooked by travelers heading for larger cities like Stockholm, Gothenburg, and Malmö, Helsingborg still boasts distinctive architecture, a busy marina, a so-called 'tropical beach', castles, nature parks, rich history, and quaint and quirky spots to have fika. I love coming to Helsingborg for day trips or weekend getaways to relax and hang out by the beautiful marina.

A fun fact about Helsingborg: *bulle med bulle* – chokladboll in a bun – was created and made popular here and every 10 April is celebrated by eating chokladbollar with bread buns. Helsingborg loves chokladbollar as much as I do!

Quick facts from Visit Helsingborg:

- Helsingborg has 143,304 inhabitants, as of June 2018
- Helsingborg is located exactly where the Öresund straits are at their narrowest, making Helsingør in Denmark the nearest neighboring town
- Helsingborg is more than 900 years old
- Popular attractions to visit in Helsingborg are Dunkers Culture Center, the Kärnan medieval tower, Sofiero Palace and Gardens, and the Fredriksdal open-air museum
- It's only a 10-minute walk from the city center to the beach
- The free wifi-zone at Gröningen in Helsingborg is probably the largest in Europe

I recommend the quiz on the Visit Helsingborg website to help guide you on your first trip to this lovely city.

www.visithelsingborg.com

ebbas fik

Ebbas Fik is an institution in the city that loves chokladbollar and *bulle med bulle*. All the small, colorful, decorative details of this diner-konditori are from the 1950s and Swedish. Located just a couple of blocks from Helsingborg Central Station, Ebbas Fik serves up excellent hamburgers, sandwiches, pastries, and classic sodas but without any Americana, as is often the norm in American-influenced diners. Walking in there, it felt like both a time warp and a Swedish-American exchange program… quirky and special.

Ebba, the owner, is a friendly outspoken character, with a sweet tooth and a surplus of creative energy. In the emails leading up to our first meeting, I took on the challenge of trying all the different kinds of chokladbollar she serves. She said it would be quite a task to try them all, and after one look at the sheer size of her large chokladbollar I knew I was going to struggle. She serves five different varieties of large chokladbollar – banana, mint, orange, rum, and classic – all made without milk, nuts or gluten. In our conversations, Ebba said her customers kept on listing their food allergies so she decided to make the balls without any troublesome ingredients.

I ended up choosing the mint, orange, and rum chokladbollar, and took large bites out of each ball. The smooth, sweet texture of the balls was so delicate. With a cheeky glint in her eyes, Ebba said, "I'm not sharing the recipe, it's my secret!" Annoying, but I totally understand.

We discussed the importance of proportions and temperature requirements in getting the chokladbollar just the right texture. Though chokladbollar are one of the first things most Swedes learn to make, they still require trial and error to develop something lagom.

www.ebbasfik.se

fahlmans konditori

'Kärt barn har många namn'
A love child has many names

Walking up the street from the majestic Helsingborg City Hall is Fahlmans Konditori, located at the corner of the busy main shopping street. This traditional bakery and café has been a Helsingborg mainstay for generations. In the city that consumes the most chokladbollar, I met up with Max Fahlman, the son of the owner, who has been at the helm of bringing back *bulle med bulle* through creating a video of himself celebrating his childhood habit of eating a chokladboll inside a bread bun… it went viral. He and his friends have had a lot of support from the press to make a bulle med bulle day and indeed, April 11 is now national bulle med bulle day!

Max is not your usual inheritor of a family business and is making his own career apart from, but connected to, Fahlmans Konditori. He met me for fika here, just before the winter afternoon turned to dusk. Beanie-clad Max had just come from his construction job. Winters bring people inside and it was very busy that afternoon. Most of the items behind the counter were finished or fast disappearing. Traditional Swedish pastries like chokladbollar, *prinsesstårta*, *dammsugare*, *kladdkaka*, *semlor*, and *fikabröd* were especially popular.

He ordered a bun and a chokladboll to create a bulle med bulle right in front of me. Cutting the bun in half and making a little hole to place the ball in, Max then squished the bread to make a chokladboll burger. We halved the simple sandwich and I took my first bite. The crunch from the bun and the chocolate in the middle felt like I was eating a rudimentary rendition of *pain au chocolat*. School aged children would order this if they were hungry because it was cheap, yummy, and easy to assemble.

www.fahlmans.se

lund

Lund, a small university city in the heart of Southern Sweden, with some of the most educated residents in the country, is the perfect location for tons of cozy konditoris. A short train ride from Malmö, this historic city of Lund also boasts über cute architecture, an iconic cathedral, ivy-covered university buildings, cobblestone streets and a diverse population. The city is quaint and a pleasant little retreat from larger urban areas. It has a friendly, communal atmosphere that seems built for intellectual conversations over copious cups of strong black coffee.

Lund University is the oldest university in Scandinavia and its campus dominates the entire makeup of the city. Other sights worth visiting are the Lund Cathedral, which houses an astronomical clock, large pillars, and an architecture that rivals Barcelona's Sagrada Familia (in my opinion)! I love spending time in this quiet city to catch up with friends, read, write, or just wander down the cute cobblestone streets.

Visit Lund's tourist information office is conveniently located right by the Lund Central Station and can provide you a guide to direct you to the best spots in the city.

Recommended by Visit Lund as the top places to go in Lund:

- Lund Cathedral: Sweden's most visited church, with over 700,000 visitors each year. Among the Cathedral's many attractions is the astronomical clock, dating back to 1424. The clock plays daily at 12 noon (1 pm on Sunday) and 3 pm
- Kulturen is an open air-museum consisting of two blocks filled with historic houses and gardens. Step into the houses and experience the life of the city and the country from the Middle Ages to the 1930s
- The Museum of Sketches is a unique art museum with a focus on the artistic process and art in public space. The museum's collections include international masters like Henri Matisse, Sonia Delaunay and Henry Moore
- Vattenhallen Science Centre is a place where children and adults can experience interactive experiments and participate in interactive exhibitions
- The Botanical Garden has existed in Lund since 1690. Around 1860 it was moved to its present location and today there are over 7,000 species of plant, grown on eight hectares (20 acres) in the heart of Lund
- Lund University Historical Museum is the second largest archaeological museum in Sweden with finds from the Stone, Bronze and Iron ages, as well as medieval art from Scania

www.visitlund.se

love coffee roasters

What happens when you combine wine with coffee? … love! Love Coffee Roasters in Lund is the brainchild of Daniel Remheden, originally a sommelier before he discovered the nuances and delicate flavors of well-brewed coffee. For the past 17 years, he's been roasting coffee beans and creating a local fanbase. I had the pleasure of meeting Daniel and talking about his humble beginnings, as well as discussing coffee cupping (known to the non-initiated as coffee tasting).

Love Coffee Roasters is a cute little place with an outdoor patio at the back for everyone to enjoy his or her fika al fresco. Buttery croissants, fluffy cardamom and cinnamon buns, and super-nuanced vegan chokladbollar are also offered at this charming establishment. Daniel mentions that all his pastries and chokladbollar are the fruit of partnerships with nearby bakeries. His philosophy with his café is to create a sense of community by working together to make Lund a unique destination for food and beverages.

When I took a bite into the vegan chokladboll, I was blown away by the dark chocolate and coffee flavors. Daniel said that he gets his batch from the small vegan place "around the corner" called Cashew. The coffee used in Cashew's chokladbollar is, of course, from Love Coffee Roasters.

I spent quite a number of afternoons here typing on my laptop while sipping the day's filter coffee, since the ambience and coziness of the place promoted a feeling of productivity. This is certainly the perfect place for Lund University students to linger, to study, to enjoy some really good specialty coffee, or just to have a fika with a classmate and recharge.

www.lovecoffee.se

ramklints

The scents of butter and coffee wafted through the air as I walked in the entrance of Ramklints Café and Conditori, in the center of Lund. Here I met with operations manager Anna. Being also the daughter of the owners behind this family-run business, Anna literally grew up here, so running a konditori is second nature.

Anna talked about her childhood rolling chokladbollar in the bakery and pouring sugar into the cake mixes, and how she slowly worked her way up from behind the counter to the back-end of operations. The tradition of fika is well embedded in Swedish culture, but nowhere is it more alive than in Ramklints. On that cold grey morning, I noticed that most of the patrons having their breakfast or mid-morning fika were from an older generation. Most of them stopped by our table to greet Anna, evidently well-worn regulars.

As we sat there by the window, with cold winter rain beating down outside, Anna started talking about what she loves most about fika.

"It's such a good trend because it makes a change from going to the bar," she said. "You can hang out here and just sit and talk. We don't have loud music. Here, it's just you and your friends with a cup of coffee and a cinnamon bun, chokladbollar or *wienerbröd* (Danish pastry)."

The care and attention required to know the regulars by name at this traditional konditori is evidenced by the stream of people who frequent it. Having a fika is all about recharging in the company of friends. Ramklints is that relaxed place in the middle of the big square in central Lund where one goes to eat yummy pastries, drink coffee, and receive warm hospitality.

www.ramklints.se

malmö

Multicultural and eclectic, Malmö's landscape is changing at a rapid pace. An influx of immigrants, expats, global companies, tech startups, a food scene embracing global flavors, and a plethora of ethnic neighborhoods all characterize this city in the south of Sweden. Walking the streets of Malmö, you'll hear all kinds of languages being spoken.

Malmö is Sweden's third largest city and the most populous in South Sweden. It's accessible by train in less than 20 minutes from Copenhagen thanks to the Öresund bridge, which connects Sweden to Denmark (the Öresund bridge was made famous by the Nordic crime drama TV series *The Bridge*). The city's close proximity to the rest of Europe means it's no surprise Malmö is rapidly transforming into an international hub. A quaint city center that hosts annual festivals like the *Malmöfestivalen* and Christmas markets, but modern Malmö is host to a mix of global offices for international companies, coworking spaces, traditional Swedish businesses, and trendy coffee roasteries.

Malmö Town, the official website for the city of Malmö, lists what you can do, eat, and see in the city, as well as hosting an events calendar.

Top attractions in Malmö:

- Gamla Stad: The old town area is within walking distance of the central station
- Västra Hamnen: Coastal western part of the city, with sweeping views of the Öresund Bridge and a public sauna near Riberborgstranden
- Öresund Bridge: The bridge between Sweden and Denmark was made famous by the Nordic noir TV crime series, *The Bridge*
- Kungsparken: The centrally located park by the *Slottsparken* filled with greenery
- Malmö Museum: Located inside a castle fortress, this is a *must do* for first time visitors to Malmö and the Skåne region
- Moderna Museum Malmö: A smaller version of Stockholm's Modern Museum but more experimental and with changing exhibitions
- Teknikens Och Sjöfartens Hus (Technical and Seaman's house): Museum with hands-on maritime and technology displays, including a climb-aboard WWII-era submarine
- Malmö Konstmuseum (Malmö Art Museum): The museum houses major collections of Nordic modern and contemporary art

www.malmotown.com

djäkne kaffebar

Finding a coworking space that serves great coffee and has a fast wifi connection is always a challenge when I'm on the road. Djäkne kaffebar in Malmö offers the perfect combination of all three. With its minimalist, clean Swedish décor, specialty coffee from the Nordic region, lots of tables, plug sockets, friendly baristas, and a central location, what's not to like about this space?

Djäkne is part coffee shop and part coworking space. It's equipped with meeting rooms and they offer memberships as part of their initiative for supporting budding entrepreneurs and startups in Malmö. The startup scene in Malmö is burgeoning, and so is the specialty coffee that goes along with it! Malmö's proximity to Copenhagen, and Europe in general, makes it easy to see why Malmö is becoming an exciting place to work and live, and Djäkne are capitalizing on that trend.

I met with Marvin Bonsen, manager of operations at Djäkne. He's an innovative person with a passion for enhancing both the fika and start up scenes in Malmö. He and his team of forward-thinking baristas are probably the reason why this place is popular in Malmö. Originally from The Netherlands, Bonsen talks about the winters being 'dark and gloomy' in Sweden. Nevertheless, the café is always busy in the winter, with many people looking for spaces to work and escape from the harsh weather.

On a personal level, I really liked Djäkne for the rotation of coffees they feature from specialty roasters in the Nordic regions. I also love the open space, the knowledgeable baristas, and the quiet work environment. This is a place I keep returning to in Malmö.

www.djakne.com

bloggers

lola akinmade åkerström

The busy morning rush hour at Stockholm Central Station buzzed around me as I rushed to meet the illustrious and radiant Lola Akinmade Åkerström. Lola greeted me with a big warm smile and a hug as she helped me with my bags into a calm café away from the busy station. Dressed all in black, her hair loose and curly, it wasn't hard to miss this inspiring travel writer and photographer.

I had been reading her articles for several years now in *Afar* magazine and National Geographic, as well as on her own website www.slowtravelstockholm.com, so I felt a bit intimidated about meeting her. Her low-key vibe put me at ease almost instantly. Lola has been an expat based in Stockholm for more than a decade now, and she knows the ins and outs of living in Swedish society, while retaining her Nigerian roots and American culture.

Lola said she's embraced the Swedish culture of fika, lagom, and the law of *Jante* (that frowns upon any kind of boasting or showing off) into her life, thanks to her Swedish husband.

"My husband's Swedish and I leave the baking all to him," said Lola. "He's really good at that. He makes really good chocolate balls, *kardemummabulle*, and cinnamon buns."

Lola's all-time favorite, however, is the *kardemummabulle* from a small bakery on the island of Lidingö just outside Stockholm city.

Having recently published a book about lagom, I had to ask Lola what her personal thoughts on lagom were.

"Lagom is the Swedish ethos and philosophy of life," she responded. "Lagom is living your most optimal life. It's a personal decision. My lagom is different than, say, your lagom."

At the heart of it, Lola explained that lagom is about taking out "the excess that you don't need in your life because it causes stress."

I couldn't agree more.

Follow Lola and her travel stories at www.lolaakinmade.com

pierre orsander

Behind the Swedish blog www.skitgott.se is Pierre Orsander. Pierre is a passionate, active food blogger based in Malmö, who focuses on the food scenes in Malmö, Lund, Gothenburg, and Stockholm, but has also branched out to other cities within the Nordic region. A regular at food and beverage events, he also runs a monthly Fika AW (Fika After Work) event.

"Food is not only what you eat; it's what you see, feel, and how it makes *you* feel," commented Pierre when we met on a balmy, cloudy and cold winter day in a cozy fika café in central Malmö. He went on to add, "comfort food makes you feel warm."

Food is Pierre's passion, but he is also passionate about meeting other people and sharing knowledge. An avid traveler and foodie, Pierre searches for new experiences that change his perspective on what food is, what it can be, and what it could be.

Pierre is also, unsurprisingly, fascinated by coffee. Just as with food, he likes to mix it up and try new experiences. His current coffee crush is Ethiopian coffee for its delicate fruit and floral nuances of flavor. He grew up typically Swedish, however, drinking a traditionally strong, almost burnt, Skåne roast.

Coffee and food are longstanding partners in Sweden, coming together to create the perfect fika. According to Pierre, fika is a perfect example of food and coffee partnering up to create a truly memorable experience: fika is a time for reflection, either solo or with friends and family. According to Pierre, "You don't do fika stressed out."

And it is these experiences that keep Pierre motivated to keep on sharing. "It makes me happy when other people are happy because they have a new food or coffee experience," he said.

Follow Pierre at:
@skitgott (Instagram)
www.skitgott.se
www.pierreorsander.com

fika på svenska
glossary: swedish for *fika*

Baka	Baking
Bryggkaffe	Black filter coffee
Bulle med bulle/ Bulle i bulle	A ball with/ in a bun. A popular snack for school aged children is to have a big chokladbollar smashed in between two halves of a bread bun. Popularized in Helsingborg, Sweden, and recently enjoying a comeback
Bullmamma	The stereotypical image of a mother and ideal female figure who spends all of her time in the kitchen cooking and baking for her children
Choklad	Chocolate
Chokladbollar	Swedish Chocolate balls made with oats but paired perfectly with coffee for a fika
Dammsugare/ punschrulle	Directly translated as vacuum cleaner, but these are marzipan confections made with leftover cake fillings and a food colored green marzipan
Delicatobollar	A brand of chokladbollar that is manufactured and sold for the masses, usually found in the grocery stores throughout Sweden
Dricka kaffe på bit	When you put the sugar cube in between your teeth and keep it there while sipping your black coffee
En bagatelle	A frivolous disagreement or a small crisp bread snack
En kopp fika	A cup of coffee
Enkel/ Dubbel espresso	Single or Double espresso
Fett najs	A Stockholm specific regional slang for saying that is 'fat nice'

Fika	A play on the Swedish word for coffee, from *kaffe* to *fäka*, which then became 'fika' – slang for taking a coffee break
Fik	A place to have fika
Fikapaus	Taking a break to have fika
Fikarast	A specific time to break for fika
Fikarum	A break room for the purpose of having a fika
Fikaställe	A place to have fika
Fikastund	The moment you have a fika
Fikasugen	A fika craving
Goda	Good, yummy, delicious
Grädde	Cream, whether its whipped or pouring cream
Godis	Candy. Especially the pick and mix variety found in grocery stores through Sweden. Traditionally, parents would only allow chilren to have candy on Saturday, called lördagsgodis
Hemgjorda/ Hembakat	Homemade or home baked
Kafferep	Literally means 'coffee rope' and is a word used for organizing a get together over coffee and cookies
Kakao (pulver)	Cocoa, cocoa powder
Kakmonster	Someone who has an extreme sweet tooth and *loves* cookies
Kanelbullar/ Kanelbulle	Cinnamon buns plural and singular. Typically eaten at a fika. These cinnamon buns are not like the American versions. Instead of icing for a topping, pearl sugar is used
Kardemummabullar/ Kardemummabulle	Cardamom buns plural and singular. Also a typical sweet bun to eat at a *fika*. A bit spicier than a cinnamon bun
Kladdkaka	A Swedish gooey chocolate cake that is popular with a dollop of cream or dusting of icing sugar and found in fika cafes throughout Sweden

Kola	A type of Swedish caramel fudge but slightly different
Laga (mat)	Cooking or preparing food
Lagom	A Swedish way of life to describe a balance. Not too much, not too *little, just right*
Latte	Espresso with steamed milk
Lattemorsor/ Lattemamma	Mothers on maternity leave that walk around with their babies in the strollers while drinking coffee. Could also be used to stereotype a group of mothers
Lattepappa	Fathers who have coffee with their babies at cafés before heading to the nearest park
Mellanmål	Between meals
Mjölkchoklad	Milk chocolate
Mörk choklad	Dark chocolate
Mysigt	A cozy feeling but you can also use it to describe a cozy time for example *fredagsmys* literal translation 'Friday cozy'
Pärlsocker	Pearl Sugar that is often found on top of chokladbollar, kanelbulle, cookies, cakes. You can find pearl sugar in specialty baking shops outside of Scandinavia but is a very common ingredient found in grocery stores throughout Scandinavia and Finland
Påtår, or Påtag/ Tretår	Refill of coffee and a second refill
Sju sorters kakor	Seven different types of small cookies and cakes. A Swedish traditional Sunday *fika* at the grandparents' house, involving seven different types of small cookies or cakes
Smakar gott	Tastes good
Småkakor	Small cookies or biscuits
Smör	Butter

index

alaine's araksbollar	47
alaine's classic swedish chokladbollar recipe	53
all about almonds and hazelnuts	83
almond loveballs	81
an apple ball a day…	63
aunt mona's rum balls	45
black forest cherry	39
blue balls	65
boozehound whisky bourbon balls	41
bougie balls	55
candy cane *jultidschokladbollar*	91
chocolate salty caramel balls	93
classic white	59
danish rum balls (*rømkugle*)	43
earl grey	101
fudgy chocolate	95
guinness balls	49
kokos kokos coconuts *kaya*	103
make me blue-tiful antioxidant balls	67
monkey balls	69
gimme my nutty balls	85
pistache	87
razzle dazzle raspberry	71
s'mores chokladbollar	107
strawberry fields of chocolate morsels	73
swedish *kanelbullebollar* cinnamon balls	109
vegan classic	57
vegan monkey balls	75
white lemon *dröm*	77
zen tea ceremony with matcha	111

tack så mycket till acknowledgements

I'd like to thank all my ball-eating friends and family, from my earliest experiments to my latest and craziest combinations. From Sweden and Singapore, to Brussels, the Swiss Alps, Oulu, London, Malta, the Netherlands, Sydney, and everywhere else in between!

Allie and The Ground Malmö
Anna and Ramklints Konditori
Daniel and Love Coffee Roasters
Marvin and Victoria and Djäkne Kaffebar
Pierre Orsander
Ebba and Ebbas Fik
Max and Fahlmans Konditori
Felicia and Alkemisten
Mimmi and Brogyllen
Pernilla and Da Matteo
Cymon and Gast Café, Kaffeverket, Snickarbacken 7
Lola Akinmade Åkerström
Visit Lund
Visit Helsingborg
Visit Göteborg
Visit Stockholm
Visit Sweden
ScandAsia
Sabrina and Krakakoa chocolate
Jo Parfitt, Joshua Parfitt, Sam Parfitt, Jack Scott, Ginny Philps

Special thanks to Mom, Dad and Alicia for supporting my crazy ideas and testing my kitchen experiments.

Ivan, Ingolf, and little Tunisia for your hospitality and letting me make copious amounts of chokladbollar in your kitchen.

And of course my biggest ball-eating fanatic friends (you know who you are!)…

Tackar!

Ska vi fika?

Smörgås	An open-faced sandwich
Socker	Sugar
Sylt	Jam or preserves. Usually berries like lingonberries, strawberries, blueberries, cloudberries
Tack så mycket	Thank you very much. You can also use *Tack* or *Tackar*
Tårta	A tart or cake
Tryffel	Truffle
Vit choklad	White chocolate

www.ingramcontent.com/pod-product-compliance
Lightning Source LLC
Chambersburg PA
CBHW040759240426
43673CB00014B/389